T0330111

Unpacking Innovation

Unpacking Innovation
Corporate Dynamics, Business Models and
Digital Technologies

Marco Cucculelli

*Department of Economics and Social Sciences,
Marche Polytechnic University, Italy*

 Edward Elgar
PUBLISHING

Cheltenham, UK • Northampton, MA, USA

The book contains the results of a research program supported by the Fondazione Cariverona. Project title: IT-compliant business models for technology transfer and system optimization – Project ID 0498 - # 9215 – Bando Ricerca Scientifica – Principal investigator: Prof Marco Cucculelli (Università Politecnica delle Marche, Ancona, Italy)

Published by
Edward Elgar Publishing Limited
The Lypiatts
15 Lansdown Road
Cheltenham
Glos GL50 2JA
UK

Edward Elgar Publishing, Inc.
William Pratt House
9 Dewey Court
Northampton
Massachusetts 01060
USA

A catalogue record for this book
is available from the British Library

Library of Congress Control Number: 2024932692

This book is available electronically in the **Elgar**online
Economics subject collection
http://dx.doi.org/10.4337/9781035327461

ISBN 978 1 0353 2745 4 (cased)
ISBN 978 1 0353 2746 1 (eBook)

Printed and bound by CPI Group (UK) Ltd, Croydon, CR0 4YY

Contents

Contributors

Riccardo Cappelli: Department of Economics and Social Science, Marche Polytechnic University, Ancona, Italy

Marco Chiaromonte: Department of Economics and Social Science, Marche Polytechnic University

Marco Cucculelli: Department of Economics and Social Science, Marche Polytechnic University, Ancona, Italy

Blendi Gerdoçi: Management Department, Faculty of Economy, University of Tirana, Tirana, Albania

Noemi Giampaoli: Department of Economics and Social Science, Marche Polytechnic University, Ancona, Italy

Daniela Lena: Department of Economics and Social Science, Marche Polytechnic University, Ancona, Italy

Silvia Leoni: School of Business and Economics, Maastricht University, Maastricht, Netherlands

Damiano Meloni: Department of Economics and Social Science, Marche Polytechnic University, Ancona, Italy

Jasmine Mondolo: Department of Economics and Social Science, Marche Polytechnic University, Ancona, Italy

Matteo Renghini: Department of Economics and Social Science, Marche Polytechnic University, Ancona, Italy

Introduction to *Unpacking Innovation*
Marco Cucculelli

In recent years, firms have been operating in a rapidly changing and complex environment: economic integration and cooperation have significantly increased, and so has competition. Additionally, the challenges posed by globalization intertwine with those attributable to technological change, which has been exhibiting an unprecedented degree of pervasiveness and pace of diffusion. To reap the benefits and minimize the threats stemming from such a radical technological transformation and to cope with this dynamic context, companies need to properly identify and consolidate their own resources, competencies and strategies, as well as to acquire adequate knowledge of their business environment. At the same time, they need to be ready to innovate their way of doing business in order to adapt to the changing conditions and stay competitive.

The unique set of resources, strategies, activities and relationships with stakeholders that characterize a firm defines the firm's business model. Even though there is no broad consensus on the definition, nature, structure, and other relevant aspects of this construct (Zott, Amit & Massa, 2011), academics seem to converge on viewing a business model as an interrelated sum of three 'building blocks', i.e., value creation, value delivery and value capture (Osterwalder, Pigneur & Tucci, 2005; Osterwalder & Pigneur, 2010; Teece, 2010). Business models have been mainly studied by management scholars so far, but they have been receiving growing attention and acknowledgement from the literature in economics as well. In particular, Corrado et al. (2022) argue that investments in business models should be regarded as investments in intangible capital, which in turn play a significant role for the enterprise's strategy and success. Likewise, policy makers are also increasingly interested in business models, as they have devoted increasing attention in finding effective tools to manage industrial change and support successful industrial transformation.

In this context, innovation is particularly important: established companies, especially in business contexts characterized by new and disruptive technologies, fast-evolving customer needs and new regulations, are expected to reshape, from time to time, their competitive profile to keep up with change and maintain or create competitive advantage; in other words, they need to periodically update their business models to renew the innovation ecosystem and move away from current technologies and practices. In light of these considerations, business model innovation should be added to the list of primary forms of innovation, which also includes technological innovation, social and policy innovation, and public sector innovation (OECD, 2021).

Although there exists a broad academic literature on business models and business model innovation, empirical evidence on these constructs and their link with other relevant variables is still limited. This is also partly attributable to the fact that the concept of business model is quite broad and elusive, thus leading to different definitions and measurement challenges. Also, most of the extant studies have focused on startups, for which the definition of the business profile often overlaps perfectly with the initial organizational setup and with the planned market positioning defined by the entrepreneur.

In light of these considerations, this volume aims to provide fresh evidence on the innovation and reconfiguration of the business profile carried out by incumbent firms in the current context of increasing competition, globalization and digitalization. In incumbent companies, business model innovation is generally more challenging than in new ventures: while a startup exploring a new business model may draw on a 'blank sheet' in terms of organizational design and resource allocation, an incumbent has pre-established structures, resources, and relationships that need to be reorganized, and that can discourage or hinder this process. Accordingly, this book explores the determinants and implications of business model innovation using various methodologies and data sources and devoting particular attention to the role of technological change. Its main contributions to the extant literature can be summarized as follows:

- It provides robust empirical evidence on a quite broad and elusive concept – business models;
- It empirically assesses business model innovation using different approaches and data sources, including a unique survey administered to a large sample of Italian companies;
- It focuses on incumbent firms, rather than on startups – which are the target of most of the previous literature;
- It devotes particular attention to the adoption of digital technologies, which represents a key feature of the ongoing unprecedented wave of technological change.

The book comprises eight chapters. Chapter 1, which has an introductory and qualitative stance, conducts a review of a considerable number of studies that investigate business model innovation and digital technologies (e.g., Big Data, robotics and Artificial Intelligence-related applications) in incumbent firms. Chapter 2 quantitively sheds light on the determinants of business model reconfiguration focusing on the role played by the adoption of digital technologies. To this end, it draws upon a unique survey covering several relevant aspects of firms' business profile and strategies, which we administered to a representative sample of Italian companies. The survey, which is shortly presented in the Appendix of the book, is the basic empirical tool that allowed the generation of the datasets used in the empirical analysis. Chapter 3 assesses how various firm-specific characteristics, including its green profile and the adoption of digital technologies, affect a firm's ability to capture a higher share of value in its value chain by innovating its business model. Chapter 4 further scrutinizes the link between technological change, business models and the position in the value chain by studying how the adoption of Big Data-related digital technologies influences the probability that a firm enters a niche market – a type of market segment which, according to Osterwalder's popular framework, is part of a firm's business model. Chapter 5, instead, explores the role of four types of business model innovation (BMI) in the sales' growth of high-growth companies, a distinctive feature of several competitive ecosystems. The investigation of the link between BMI and firm performance continues in Chapter 6, which assesses to what extent inter-firm heterogeneity in terms of performance is ascribable to differences in the firms' business model innovation across established firms. To this end, it builds and clusters a set of business model-related variables drawing upon financial secondary data from Aida-Bureau van Dijk and, in doing so, it shows that also a firm-level database of financial and business information can represent a useful and easily available source of information for the purpose of identifying business models.

Finally, Chapters 7 and 8 introduce an additional data source that researchers can exploit to identify business models, namely firms' websites, and present two alternative approaches aimed at retrieving information from them. In particular, Chapter 7 detects the unique set of products, technologies, competencies and know-how that shape corporate business models using rigorous text-mining techniques, and then links the selected companies based on business model similarities, which may represent the starting point for knowledge exchange and cooperation. In Chapter 8, instead, the identification of the business model at both the firm and the sectoral level for a larger number of companies was carried out by a team of analysts who manually scrutinized each company's website for about 2,000 firms. As a result, we can suggest that not only technological change does affect business models, but also helps obtain reliable and accurate evidence on this topic by providing researchers with increasing data availability and more advanced data mining and data analysis techniques.

We reckon that this book can offer some useful insights to companies that intend to adopt digital technologies and innovate their business models, as well as to researchers who are simply interested in the topic or also intend to empirically investigate it. Additionally, the book could be adopted in post-graduate courses in Industrial Organization, Industrial Economics and Economics of the Firm, the Economics of Business Strategy and related subjects.

This book would not have come about without several important contributions.

First, I would like to thank the Cariverona Foundation, which generously provided financial support for the extensive research program that produced this book. In addition to the results presented and discussed in the book, several other articles have been published – or are under review – in major international journals. The amount of scientific knowledge gained through the research program is enormous and has enabled me to share the findings in countless meetings with national and local stakeholders, policy makers, and practitioners, as well as the scientific research community at national and international conferences.

I also thank the Cariverona Foundation for giving a wonderful group of young scientists the chance to join a multidisciplinary team and pursue an ambitious research program. I believe that this was a unique opportunity for them and, hopefully, a first step in their academic careers. I would like to thank the Foundation on their behalf.

The research program might have not been even started without the generous and smart contribution of Marco Chiaromonte, who led the surveys from the beginning and managed the datasets throughout the program. Similarly, the book might have not come to fruition without the passionate, dedicated, and brilliant work of Jasmine Mondolo, who compiled all the research material into a beautiful and fluid editorial product. I would also like to thank all the contributors whose various roles and contributions helped to make the book a reality: Riccardo Cappelli, Marco Chiaromonte, Blendi Gerdoçi, Noemi Giampaoli, Daniela Lena, Silvia Leoni, Damiano Meloni, Jasmine Mondolo and Matteo Renghini.

A special thanks goes to my family, who has lent me its unconditional support and precious time, that I have to give back. And to my father for his curiosity and love for discovery.

REFERENCES

Corrado, C., Haskel, J., Jona-Lasinio, C. and Iommi, M. (2022). Intangible Capital and Modern Economies. *Journal of Economic Perspectives*, 36(3), 3–28.
OECD (2021), Regional Innovation in Piedmont, Italy: From Innovation Environment to Innovation Ecosystem, OECD Regional Development Studies, OECD Publishing, Paris, https://doi.org/10.1787/7df50d82-en.

Osterwalder, A. and Pigneur, Y. (2010). *Business Model Generation: A Handbook for Visionaries, Game Changers, and Challengers.* John Wiley and Sons, Inc., Hoboken, New Jersey.

Osterwalder, A., Pigneur, Y. and Tucci, C.L. (2005). Clarifying Business Models: Origins, Present, and Future of the Concept. *Communications of the Association for Information Systems*, 16(1), 1–25.

Teece, D.J. (2010). Business Models, Business Strategy and Innovation. *Long Range Planning*, 43(2–3), 172194.

Zott, C., Amit, R. and Massa, L. (2011). The Business Model: Recent Developments and Future Research. *Journal of Management*, 37(4), 1019–1042.

1. Digital technologies and business model innovation in incumbent firms: a systematic review

Noemi Giampaoli, Matteo Renghini and Marco Cucculelli

1. INTRODUCTION

Digital technologies (hereafter, DTs) are particularly relevant for business model innovation (hereafter, BMI) in incumbent companies, as the process of transforming existing business models in companies that have already established themselves in a particular industry structure can be critical (Bowman et al., 2019; Kiel et al., 2017).

A significant strand of literature has addressed the issue of how innovation and the adoption of DTs change the way companies do business (Fakhar et al., 2020);[1] however, the extant literature is quite heterogeneous, and evidence on the link between DTs and BMI in incumbent firms is still limited. This chapter aims to provide a comprehensive overview of the extant research, and focuses on how the adoption of digital technologies affects business model adaptation and innovation in incumbent firms. To this end, we conduct a systematic literature review: first, after a preliminary analysis of the recent literature, we identified a wide range of potential terms that could be associated with the three main topics of interest, i.e., "digital technologies", "business model innovation", and "existing/incumbent/established companies". The selected sets of keywords used in Scopus in July 2023 are the following:

("digital" OR "hi-tech" OR "high tech" OR "4.0" OR "digital technology" OR "digitalization" OR "digital transformation" OR "digitalizations" OR

---

[1]   Scholars have clustered DTs into three main conceptualizations: digital transformation (Caputo et al., 2016; Kotarba, 2018; Li, 2018; Schallmo et al., 2017; Verhoef et al., 2021), Internet of Things (IoT) (Dijkman et al., 2015; Caputo et al., 2016; Kiel et al., 2017; Bresciani et al., 2018), and Industry 4.0 (Müller et al., 2018; Vial, 2019; Kumar et al., 2020).

"industry 4.0" OR "industr* 4.0" OR "digital servitization" OR "technology innovation" OR "digital entrepreneurship" OR "digital technologies" OR "digital innovation" OR "digitisation" OR "digitization" OR "Internet of things" OR "IoT" OR "Industrial Internet of Things" OR "e-business");

(i)   AND ("business model innovation" OR "business model change" OR "business model*" OR "innovative business model" OR "digital business model" OR "business model transformation");

(ii) AND ("incumbent*" OR "establish" OR "established" OR "mature" OR "existing firms" OR "existing" OR "incumbent firm*" OR "incumbent adaptation").[2]

To refine our article search, we set the following parameters in the Scopus database: (i) "articles only", and (ii) "articles written in English". Given the broad range of topics covered by each literature stream, we also applied filters to restrict the analysis to the field of economics and business; specifically, we narrowed our search by selecting the following subject areas included in Scopus: (i) Economics, Econometrics, and Finance and (ii) Business, Management, and Accounting.

After that, we conducted a content analysis that unfolds through three main phases. In the first phase, we outline the main contributions in each of the three macro areas, i.e., digital technologies, business model innovation and incumbent firms, and attempt to provide a brief description of each macro area. In the second phase, we explore and analyse the relevant issues that arise from the overlaps between pairs of research macro areas; by using the above-mentioned sets of keywords and combining macro areas, we identify and discuss the key aspects of three different sub-streams: (i) digital technologies in business model innovation, (ii) digital technologies in incumbent firms, and (iii) business model innovation in incumbent firms. Finally, we focus on the intersection of the three aforementioned macro streams, which represents the core of our review; specifically, we identify the relevant papers (82 articles published between 2002 and 2023 and retrieved from Scopus in July 2023) that address the relationship between digital technologies and business model innovation in incumbent firms.

We find that DTs influence BMI in incumbent firms through all three lines of innovation identified in the business model literature, i.e., (i) value creation, (ii) value proposition, and (iii) value capture. Digital transformation enables strategic renewal and continuous adaptation of capabilities in incumbent companies, leading to improved operational efficiency and information transpar-

---

[2]   The symbol "*" allows the inclusion of all variations of the word. For example, "industr*" states for "industry" or "industries", etc.

ency. In addition, Industry 4.0 technologies facilitate real-time data exchange along the supply chain, benefiting both customers and suppliers; likewise, DTs empower existing businesses to transform and enable the development of new, highly customized products and services. DTs also have a significant impact on the value proposition: Data mining and analytics enable incumbents to develop innovative offerings, and additive manufacturing technologies help meet new market demands. Finally, digital technologies facilitate connectivity between companies, enabling greater customer reach and more efficient contracting in incumbents. As a result, the adoption of digital technologies can lead to a competitive advantage by increasing value capture even through the traditional business model.

The remainder of the chapter is organized as follows. Section 2 provides an overview of the pertinent literature. Section 3 examines the main contributions of the three sub-sectors that emerged from the overlap of the basic areas. Section 4 concludes.

2.   BMI AND DIGITAL TECHNOLOGIES: AN OVERVIEW

An increasing number of scholars have addressed the issue of business model innovation as a tool for managing organizational change and maintaining competitiveness (Saebi et al., 2017; Demil and Lecocq, 2010). Because the business model is significantly dependent on contextual factors (e.g., technology, competition, regulatory laws), scholars have focused on the role of technology and innovation in supporting business renewal and maintaining competitiveness (Chesbrough, 2010; Teece, 2010). Therefore, research on new business processes has begun to pay attention to the role of DTs as enablers of operational efficiency, innovation, and access to information. In our analysis of the collected articles, we found 2,091 articles published between 1994 and 2023 that address this topic (Figure 1.1), i.e., the overlap between these two research areas. Out of these articles, 1,413 documents were published in the last five years (i.e., between 2018 and 2023), thus highlighting the current interest in this research area.

After identifying these two research strands, we focused on established organizations, rather than startups or new ventures. In restricting our analysis to incumbents, two additional intersections emerge, as shown in Figure 1.1. The first one relates to the literature that has examined how BMI unfolds in existing firms. Based on the results obtained, we found 266 papers that addressed this topic (published between 2000 to 2023), with increased attention since 2017. The second intersection includes papers that address the role of DTs in existing companies. The results show 405 papers from 1996 to 2023, with a preponderance of publications from 2019.

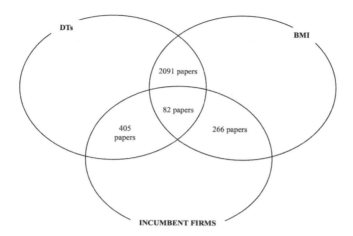

Figure 1.1   Digital technologies, incumbent firms and business model innovation

Finally, the core of the analysis results from the triple overlap of the previous two research areas, i.e., BMI and DTs, with the area of 'established firms'. The resulting cluster, comprising 82 papers published between 2002 and 2023, is discussed in the thematic analysis (Section 3) after a brief analysis of the three macro streams.

2.1   Business Model Innovation

In the literature on business models (BMs) (Teece, 2010; Osterwalder et al., 2005; Taran et al., 2015; Gassmann et al., 2014), the focus has gradually shifted from conceptualizing business models to a transformative approach that better captures the process of business model innovation (BMI) in organizations (Saebi et al., 2017). This evolution is consistent with the lack of conceptual clarity that characterized initial BM research (Casadesus-Masanell and Zhu, 2013; Schneider and Spieth, 2013). However, in the last decade, research on BMs has evolved from static descriptions to a more dynamic perspective that emphasizes business model development and innovation, leading to the concept of business model innovation (Chesbrough, 2010; Demil and Lecocq, 2010; Teece, 2010). Nowadays, scholars consider BMI as a critical source of competitive advantage in an increasingly changing envi-ronment (Casadesus-Masanell and Zhu, 2013; Amit and Zott, 2001), as well as a crucial determinant of firm performance (Chesbrough and Rosenbloom,

2002; Cucculelli and Bettinelli, 2015) and survival post-crisis, lowering the probability of default (Cucculelli and Peruzzi, 2020).

However, BMI still suffers from the original lack of conceptual clarity, and several definitions have been proposed (Casadesus-Masanell and Zhu, 2013; Foss and Saebi, 2017, 2018; Schneider and Spieth, 2013). To date, BMI has been defined in several ways: (i) as the discovery of a fundamentally different BM within an existing organization (Markides, 2006), (ii) as the search for new logics and approaches to revenue generation (Casadesus-Masanell and Ricart, 2010), and (iii) as a deliberate and observable change in the BM elements and/or architecture of an organization (Foss and Saebi, 2017; Sorescu et al., 2011; Bucherer et al., 2012; Khanagha et al., 2014; Santos et al., 2009).

The above-mentioned definitions take into account several perspectives of analysis. First, BMI represents a dynamic process in which firms seek to maintain their competitive advantage by changing activities and functions within their existing BMs. Second, BMI enables firms to explore new architectural designs that provide new opportunities related to the adoption of new technologies in value creation, distribution, and capture (Foss and Saebi, 2017; Sorescu et al., 2011); specifically, Foss and Saebi (2015, 2018) define BMI as designed, novel, and nontrivial changes to key elements of an organization's business model and the architecture that connects those elements. Third, BMI is also understood as a process (Christensen et al., 2016; Frankenberger et al., 2013) that creates new value for customers and generates higher profits (Cliffe and McGrath, 2011). Finally, BMI can be either a simple or a complex process (Taran et al., 2015), where the degree of complexity is measured by the number of building blocks that are modified or changed during the business model innovation process (Taran et al., 2015; Foss and Saebi, 2017; Yeager and Shenhar, 2019). Meanwhile, Foss and Saebi (2017) highlighted several ambiguities related to the BMI construct. For example, BMI has been studied both dynamically, as an organizational change process including capabilities, leadership, and learning mechanisms (Berends et al., 2016; Demil and Lecocq, 2010), and statically, namely as an outcome, i.e., an innovative business model within the industry.

2.2   Digital Technologies

The term 'digital technology' has attracted a great deal of attention, both among practitioners and in academia, and in a variety of research areas and disciplines ranging from engineering to information systems and management (Fitzgerald et al., 2013).[3]

DTs can be classified into three main areas based on their potential impact on the structure and behaviour of the company, which also refers to the 'building blocks' of the business model. These areas are: (i) Digital Technologies in Organization and Management, such as Enterprise Resource Planning (ERP) software; (ii) Digital Technologies in Marketing and Sales, such as social media marketing and websites; and (iii) Digital Technologies in Manufacturing, such as Production Cost Management (PCM) or Product Lifecycle Management (PLM) software (Rachinger et al., 2019; Ibarra et al., 2018; Bollweg et al., 2019; Osterwalder and Pigneur, 2010; Gassman et al., 2014; Taran et al., 2015). Moreover, most of the literature refers to DTs to study digital transformation (Caputo et al., 2016; Kotarba, 2018; Li, 2018; Schallmo et al., 2017; Verhoef et al., 2021), in addition to the Internet of Things (IoT)[4] (Dijkman et al., 2015; Caputo et al., 2016; Kiel et al., 2017; Bresciani et al., 2018) and Industry 4.0[5] (Müller et al., 2018; Vial, 2019; Kumar et al., 2020). Digital transformation is seen as a much more profound change than mere process or system updates, such as the IoT and Industry 4.0, including how existing companies may need to transform to compete and thrive in today's business environment (Libert et al., 2016). For manufacturing companies, digital transformation represents an adoption of DTs, moving from earlier stages of manufacturing to connected, intelligent enterprises in the Industry 4.0 era (Frank et al., 2019).

2.3   Incumbent Companies

The term 'incumbent' focuses on the status of the organization, i.e., existing companies, as opposed to startups. Habtay and Holmén (2014) and Markides

---

[3]   According to Hinings et al. (2018), the term "digital" refers to the conversion of analogue information into the binary language understood by computers. Since all digital content takes the same form, it can be processed using the same technologies. This potential for digitization holds the promise of breaking the tight coupling between information types and their storage, transmission, and processing technologies (Tilson et al., 2010; Yoo et al., 2010).

[4]   IoT involves the interconnection of objects via the Internet by equipping them with sensors and actuators, enabling the development of new applications and enhancing existing ones (Dijkman et al., 2015). Notable examples of IoT applications include wearables for personal health monitoring, home controllers and security systems, smart vehicles, and automated checkout systems in retailing, among others.

[5]   Industry 4.0 refers to the use of IoT applications in industrial manufacturing (e.g., advanced manufacturing solutions, additive manufacturing or 3D printing, augmented reality, cloud-based solutions, big data, and analytics), leading to cyber-physical and intelligent systems that create value for industrial activities (Müller et al., 2018).

and Charitou (2004) argue that a clear distinction between new and old business models is difficult to observe in established firms. Several studies suggest
that established small- and medium-sized enterprises (SMEs) follow a different
path than startups and large companies when innovating their business models.
In startups, designing and testing new components of the business model are
commonly considered integral steps in the growth process (Chesbrough, 2010;
Christensen et al., 2016). In contrast, this approach is less common among
established firms, such as incumbent SMEs, where experimentation is often
viewed as time-consuming and wasteful (Liu and Bell, 2019). As a result,
scholars have shifted their attention from startups to established companies
(Chesbrough, 2010; Christensen et al., 2016) to analyse the concept of BM in
a transformative way, i.e., as a tool to manage change and innovation within
the organization (Demil and Lecocq, 2010). In this regard, incumbents with
a strong entrepreneurial orientation often develop BMIs within their established business units, or establish new units dedicated to exploiting business
opportunities. It is important to note that SMEs typically pursue BMI to gain
new competitive advantages (Anwar and Shah, 2018) by leveraging digital
technologies (Bowman et al., 2019). However, several challenges remain
in the process of BMI for established companies. These challenges may be
related to the presence of a previous business model, path dependency in
the entrepreneur's prevailing logic, hidden and tacit rules of resource setting
inherited from the previous company, or pressure for short-term results (Ciulli
and Kolk, 2019). In addition, incumbent firms often face resource and time
constraints that hinder their ability to experiment with new BMs, deploy BMI
(Bowman et al., 2019; Khanagha et al., 2014), or invest in DTs and innovation
programmes to achieve new competitive advantages (Anwar and Shah, 2018;
Barney, 1991; Bollweg et al., 2019).

3.   THEMATIC ANALYSIS

This section provides an overview of the major themes that emerge from the
literature streams described above. In particular, Section 3.1 discusses the
relationship between DTs and BMI; Section 3.2 focuses on incumbent firms,
while Section 3.3 explores the role of DTs in incumbents. Finally, Section 3.4
addresses the core of our review, namely, the body of literature on DTs and
BMI in incumbents.

3.1   Business Model Innovation and Digital Technologies

BMI and DTs have been thoroughly explored by the recent academic literature, and a strong link between these two topics has been identified. DTs are
recognized as important enablers and supporters of BMI (Chesbrough, 2010;

Christensen et al., 2016; Ibarra et al., 2018; Moeuf et al., 2018; Bollweg et al., 2019). In particular, the adoption of DTs has been recognized as a significant driver of BMI, particularly for SMEs (Kiel et al., 2017; Christensen et al., 2016; Khanagha et al., 2014; Chesbrough, 2010; Müller et al., 2018; Baden-Fuller and Haefliger, 2013). For instance, several studies suggest that companies can use different types of DTs to facilitate, enable, or drive their BMI (Habtay and Holmén, 2014; Kiel et al., 2017; Nambisan, 2017; Ibarra et al.; 2018, Moeuf et al.; 2018, Müller et al., 2018; Anwar and Shah, 2018; Nagy et al., 2018).

To give some examples, Baden-Fuller and Haefliger (2013) and Nambisan (2017) explore the relationships between BMs, technological innovation, and entrepreneurship. While Baden-Fuller and Haefliger (2013) examine the link between BM and innovation by emphasizing their importance for firm growth, Nambisan (2017) advocates for a DT perspective of entrepreneurship. Christensen et al. (2016) and Habtay and Holmén (2014) observe that incumbent firms often struggle to effectively adapt their business models to compete with disruptive innovations. Christensen et al. (2016) emphasize the importance of BMI and highlight the challenges that incumbents face when responding to disruptive technologies. Meanwhile, Habtay and Holmén (2014) assess how incumbent firms respond to disruptive business model innovation focusing on the moderating role of technology-driven versus market-driven innovation. Also, Kiel et al. (2017), Ibarra et al. (2018), and Nagy et al. (2018) study the impact of the Industrial Internet of Things (IIoT) on BMs. In particular, Kiel et al. (2017) investigate how the IIoT affects the BM of established manufacturing companies using a business-level perspective; the authors posit that the IIoT can enable new revenue streams and value propositions by integrating DTs into traditional manufacturing processes. Ibarra et al. (2018) and Nagy et al. (2018) explore the role of Industry 4.0 and the IoT in business strategy, focusing on the transformative potential of Industry 4.0 in reshaping corporate governance and driving innovation. Their findings confirmed and emphasized the transformative potential of these technologies in shaping the value chain and improving competitiveness. Finally, Müller et al. (2018) and Moeuf et al. (2018) focus on the industrial management of SMEs and their BMI in the context of Industry 4.0: Moeuf et al. (2018) stress the role of DTs and their influence on business strategies; Müller et al. (2018), who examine SMEs' approach to adopting BMI in the Industry 4.0 framework, stress the importance of intellectual readiness and identify key success factors, namely, a clear understanding of Industry 4.0 opportunities and challenges, a strong top-management commitment, a well-defined BMI process, a focus on customer value, and a willingness to experiment and learn.

3.2   Business Model Innovation in Incumbent Firms

As previously mentioned, so far most of the academic literature has focused on BMI in the context of startups and new ventures (Amit and Zott, 2001; Zott and Amit, 2007), with little attention paid to the process of BMI in established firms (Cortimiglia et al., 2016; Foss and Saebi, 2017; Kim and Min, 2015). Nonetheless, scholars have also examined the stages of digitally driven BMI in incumbent companies and recognized that these firms are less likely to begin a digital transformation from scratch, and require, instead, a phased approach (Berman, 2012; Cozzolino et al., 2018; Khanagha et al., 2014; Latilla et al., 2021; McGrath and McManus, 2020).

In the current business landscape, characterized by increasing complexity, traditional BMs are ageing faster than ever before, especially among established companies. Consequently, BMI is increasingly being recognized as a powerful approach to help companies address increased global competition and dynamic environmental conditions (Johnson et al., 2008; Sosna et al., 2010).

According to the existing literature, established companies have a higher likelihood to adapt their existing BMs rather than creating entirely new ones; for instance, Cozzolino et al. (2018) and Egfjord and Sund (2020) address the relationship between a firm's adaptation and its BM and introduce the concept of 'business model adaptation' to describe the changes that incumbent firms make to their BMs. Specifically, Egfjord and Sund (2020) focus on how incumbents adapt their BMs in response to variations in the external business environment, and remark that adaptability is a critical factor for both business growth and long-term survival. In addition, Pateli and Giaglis (2005) analyse in depth the role of technological change in the adaptation of business models of incumbent firms, and show how Information and Communications Technology (ICT) generates growth opportunities for BMIs.

However, creating a radically new BM for a new venture and modifying an existing BM for an established firm differ in terms of the type and intensity of innovation required (Cortimiglia et al., 2016). First of all, BMI seems to be more complex for established companies than for new ventures or startups (Foss and Saebi, 2017). Startups exploring new BMs often have fewer constraints in terms of organizational design and resource allocation, while established companies have already established structures, resources, and relationships (Egfjord and Sund, 2020). For this reason, it has proven beneficial to identify the variables that may promote BMI. Foss and Saebi (2017) identify firm type (new or established), firm age (young or old), and technological level of firm operations (traditional or high-tech) as significant drivers of BMI. Aspara et al. (2013), Johnson et al. (2008), and Sosna et al. (2010) highlight two other important drivers of BMI in established firms: competitive pressure and the struggle for survival. The innovation of the BM not only helps firms maintain a competitive advantage, but also enables them to cope with corporate crises, facilitating strategic renewal. Moreover, severe crises could provide strong motivation for incumbent firms to overcome barriers to BMI by causing managers to reflect on the design of their existing BMs and the prevailing logic (Sosna et al., 2010).

More recently, Cozzolino et al. (2018) and Sund et al. (2021) have contributed to the identification of the drivers for BMI adoption in incumbent firms by highlighting the role of disruptive BMs. Indeed, the introduction of disruptive BMs by new entrants poses an external threat that forces incumbents to respond defensively by adapting their BM. Moreover, the authors emphasized how disruptive technologies facilitate incumbents' experimentation with new ways of creating and capturing value. Specifically, Sund et al. (2021) find that incumbents can establish innovation labs that play a dual role in fostering radical innovation while supporting core business operations.

Despite the potential benefits, BMI implementation in incumbent firms faces numerous challenges and obstacles that often lead to organizational rigidity. For these reasons, the literature also focuses on the cognitive factors that act as barriers to BMI (Egfjord and Sund, 2020; Foss and Saebi, 2017; Sosna et al., 2010). Managers' perceptions and interpretations of environmental threats and opportunities interact with existing organizational routines and beliefs that shape the BMI process. For example, perceptions of critical threats may negatively impact intentions to change resource structure due to emotional threat rigidity and rational reluctance to invest in a potentially unsuccessful venture (Osiyevskyy and Dewald, 2015a). In such contexts, proposing incremental rather than radical innovations can facilitate the BMI process. In addition, assets embedded in a legacy BM may hinder BMI in incumbent firms. Unlike new entrants, incumbents already possess resources that may conflict with a new BM, i.e., conflicting assets as well as assets that contribute to the functioning of the BM (Kim and Min, 2015).

Given these challenges, incumbents are expected to balance the exploitation of new BMs with the development of existing BMs (Osiyevskyy and Dewald, 2015b; Sosna et al., 2010). Achieving this balance requires a careful appraisal of the organizational structure; however, such a balance appears to be essential to enable incumbents to effectively implement and manage BMI (Egfjord and Sund, 2020).

3.3 Incumbent Firms and Digital Technologies

The emergence of specific DTs has profoundly changed the industrial landscape and brought about both opportunities and challenges for established companies. Scholars have examined the strategies and capabilities employed by incumbents in response to the rise of DTs, and in doing so have covered several topics and research strands, including firm capabilities, cognitive factors, financing, innovation, digital transformation, organizational adoption, business models, industry dynamics, and knowledge generation.

Incumbents' propensity to introduce new DTs is primarily influenced by firms' capabilities and cognitive factors. To give some examples, Tripsas and Gavetti (2000) examine the impact of digital technologies on incumbent firms and notice that firms with strong capabilities in traditional technologies often encounter inertia when adapting to these technologies; this suggests that it is often difficult, for incumbent firms, to reconfigure their existing knowledge and capabilities to effectively leverage digital innovations. Recently, Warner and Wäger (2019) have extended the earlier findings, and argued that incumbents need to use iterative experimentation, continuous learning, and organizational ambidexterity to effectively manage digital transformation. Also, Sorenson (2000) and Gerstner et al. (2013) focus on cognitive factors too; while Sorenson (2000) stresses how social networks in industrial geography and knowledge flows might influence the innovation activities of incumbent firms, Gerstner et al. (2013) show that CEO narcissism and audience engagement become critical factors in the adoption of technological discontinuities.

Similarly, incumbents might be able to use innovative technologies whose adoption also depends on the availability of financial resources; in this respect, the seminal paper by Baumol (2004) highlights the role of financial resources in enabling incumbents to invest in DTs and innovate. In a similar vein, Brown et al. (2009) highlight the importance of debt capital and external equity; venture capital and stock market financing have been shown to promote the adoption of innovation and DT in established firms. In addition, Kenney and Zysman (2019) discuss the challenges and dilemmas faced by entrepreneurial finance in the context of new technologies and shed light on the dynamics of innovation finance in established firms.

Finally, the literature has also examined industrial dynamics and the impact of DTs on innovation. Coad and Rao (2008) explore the relationship between innovation and firm growth in high-technology sectors and assert that incumbent firms in high-technology sectors should embrace digital technologies and adopt innovative practices to maintain competitiveness. More recently, Geels et al. (2016) and Metallo et al. (2018) have also looked at the socio-technical transition paths that incumbent firms should undertake when adopting DTs. In particular, Metallo et al. (2018) show that large incumbents with prior technological competencies place more emphasis on strengthening their internal capabilities, e.g., intra-group synergy, compared to young and small firms.

All in all, we can assert that incumbents need to properly navigate socio-technical transition paths, manage competing concerns, and find a balance between stability and agility to successfully implement digital innovation. In this respect, commitment, financial resources, CEO characteristics, and stakeholders play a crucial role in the adoption of digital innovations by incumbents.

3.4   Digital Technologies and Business Model Innovation in Incumbent Firms

The implementation of digital technologies is a continuous process of strategic transformation and renewal that requires incumbents to develop and continuously adapt their capabilities in order to identify, leverage, and respond to digital disruption (Warner and Wäger, 2019). The literature has shown that identifying a full BM transformation resulting from the integration of DTs is far from straightforward (Kiel et al., 2017; Li, 2018; Müller et al., 2018; Brock et al., 2019). Gruber and Koutroumpis (2013), Nambisan et al. (2018), and Grigoriou and Rothaermel (2017) examine the role of knowledge creation in incumbents' response to DTs. In particular, Gruber and Koutroumpis (2013) analyse the impact of pro-competitive regulation on the diffusion of innovation in the context of broadband networks; the authors emphasize the importance of BMs in facilitating the adoption and diffusion of DTs in incumbent firms. Nambisan et al. (2018) and Grigoriou and Rothaermel (2017) scrutinize the role of external knowledge and collaborations in facilitating the integration of DTs in incumbent BMs, and report that the greater the external knowledge, the higher the likelihood that incumbents will adopt digital innovations. Moreover, according to some studies (e.g., Khanagha et al., 2014; Zott and Amit, 2013), technological change plays a critical role in the discovery or emergence of new BMs that have the potential to significantly alter the value creation and value capture mechanisms of incumbent firms (Khanagha et al., 2014; Zott and Amit, 2013).

The characteristics of new DTs have a direct impact on the way companies conduct their business. Klos et al. (2021) present a framework for digital transformation BM that encompasses the dimensions of value proposition, value creation, and value capture. In contrast, Haftor and Costa (2021) develop a framework where value proposition, value creation and delivery, revenue model, capabilities, and customer relationships represent the five essential dimensions that incumbents can use to improve the presence of DTs in traditional BMs.

Based on these approaches, our analysis of the literature on BMI and DTs in incumbent firms follows three different research directions that currently serve as key areas of academic research on business models, namely (i) value creation, (ii) value proposition, and (iii) value capture.

Regarding the first area, empirical evidence supports the notion that digitization of processes and adoption of smart manufacturing offer transformative potential for the value creation aspect of business models in established SMEs. By leveraging DTs, such as collecting data on machine operations, task durations, and failures, companies could improve operational efficiency and increase information transparency. This digitization process leads to a wealth of data that provides valuable insights into production status and levels, enabling informed decision-making (Müller et al., 2018). Importantly, the impact of DTs extends far beyond a company's internal operations, as Industry 4.0 technologies enable real-time data exchange across the supply chain, benefiting both customers and suppliers. Bowman et al. (2019) highlight the potential of BMI to improve the performance of incumbent companies engaged in digitization, thereby strengthening their competitiveness in the digital economy. Similarly, Sund et al. (2021) examine DTs as both an opportunity and a barrier to BMI in incumbent firms, while Bollweg et al. (2019) analyse in depth the drivers and barriers to digitization focusing on the retail sector. These studies underscore the importance of digitization for incumbents and identify factors that either hinder or facilitate the process of digital transformation. Interestingly, Brenk et al. (2019) build on the findings of Bollweg et al. (2019) and focus on the issue of learning from failures in BMI; in particular, they emphasize the critical role of entrepreneurial effectuation and show that effectively resolving conflicts within decision-making processes is essential for overcoming obstacles and improving the success rate of business model innovation in established companies. More recently, Volberda et al. (2021) suggest another way to overcome cognitive barriers that hinder strategy formation, i.e., redesigning routines and introducing new organizational forms to enable effective strategy formation in the digital age.

Regarding barriers to the adoption of BMI and DTs in established firms, part of the literature focuses on the impact of DTs at the worker level. This is because not only can these technologies offset job shortages in manufacturing, but also require the development of new expertise and skills in IoT and manufacturing (Müller et al., 2018; Rachinger et al., 2019). As a result, older workers may struggle to adopt and use these technologies because they may be unfamiliar with them and reluctant to change their established work practices. Another disadvantage of Industry 4.0 technologies is the gradual destruction of manufacturing jobs through the displacement of blue- and white-collar workers (Kiel et al., 2017; Müller et al., 2018).

In addition to the impact on value creation mechanisms, much attention has been paid to how DTs affect the value proposition dimension of the business model. In particular, companies expect a significant improvement in their ability to offer new products and services in response to market needs (Bogers et al., 2016; Kiel et al., 2017; Müller et al., 2018; Rachinger et al., 2019); one way to achieve that is through the collection, processing, and management of relevant data, commonly known as data mining and analytics. These techniques could improve traceability of production and lead to the development of innovative offerings that fundamentally change the value proposition (Kiel et al., 2017). In addition, the literature recognizes the importance for incumbent companies to embrace manufacturing technologies and transform their BMs and supply chains to meet new market demands (Bogers et al., 2016) and successfully navigate this transformational phase (Khanagha et al., 2014, 2022). Moreover, DTs play a central role in facilitating the ability of incumbents to offer highly customized and high-quality products (Kiel et al., 2017; Li, 2018; Müller et al., 2018). The literature highlights that DTs enable manufacturing firms to pursue servitization, a strategic shift from a product-oriented BM to a service-oriented BM (Frank et al., 2019; Kiel et al., 2017; Kohtamäki et al., 2019; Müller et al., 2018). Following Frank and co-authors' (2019) conceptual framework for analysing manufacturing companies' adaptation to Industry 4.0, Zaki (2019) identifies four key trajectories of digital transformation, i.e., digital technology, digital strategy, customer experience, and data-driven business models; using these trajectories, Zaki (2019) outlines how companies are shaping the next generation of services and introducing novel offerings, redefining the business landscape.

Finally, the adoption of DTs could significantly improve the mechanisms of value capture within enterprises. DTs indeed strengthen the connections between firms and enable smoother interactions between suppliers and customers. This was highlighted in studies by Müller et al. (2018), Cozzolino et al. (2021), and Khanagha et al. (2022), who assert that automated online platforms enable greater customer reach, streamlined contracting processes, and customer involvement in co-design and co-engineering activities. In addition, there seems to be a coexistence between traditional BMs and new DT-enabled BMs. While traditional BMs may continue to govern the main product lines, personalized and customer-designed products are gradually taking on a more important role (Bogers et al., 2016). In particular, Hänninen et al. (2018) explore the transformative impact of multi-sided platforms in retail and report that incumbents need to adapt their BMs to take advantage of the opportunities offered by these platforms. Cozzolino et al. (2021) also address the importance of platforms in retail and examine the dynamics of collaboration and competition between incumbent manufacturers and new platforms in digital platform-based ecosystems; according to the authors incumbents need to respond strategically to the entry of new platforms in order to maintain competitiveness within the ecosystem. The adoption of a new BM, complemented by DTs, could indeed become a source of competitive advantage, leading to increased value capture through the traditional BM (Zaki, 2019), as empirically shown D'Ippolito et al. (2019) and Klos et al. (2021).

Overall, despite the recognized benefits, there are conflicting findings regarding the impact of DTs on a firm's ability to attract new customers.

Some studies, such as Li (2018) and Müller et al., (2018), argue that DTs enable firms to win new markets and customers. Other contributions embrace a different view; for instance, according to Kiel et al. (2017), innovation in the value proposition alone does not always guarantee the acquisition of new customers; rather, a deep understanding of existing customers combined with the application of IoT technologies could be critical for a better satisfaction of the customers' needs.

4.   CONCLUSIONS

The debate on business model innovation and digital technologies, fuelled by the rapid spread of digitalization across firms, has significantly evolved. However, the extant literature is quite heterogeneous, and evidence on the link between DTs and BMI in incumbent firms is still limited. This chapter aims to provide a comprehensive overview of the existing literature and to highlight the main current research questions, issues, and challenges; in doing so, it devotes particular attention to the body of literature that specifically addresses the adaptation of BMs and DTs in established companies, which present different opportunities and challenges compared to startups and new ventures. Through a systematic literature review based on a broad and exhaustive set of keywords, we first identified and examined the studies whose main object falls into the following categories: (i) business model innovation and digital technologies, (ii) business model innovation in incumbent firms, (iii) digital technologies and incumbent firms. We then moved to the core of our review by exploring the literature resulting from the intersection of the three aforementioned research streams, namely, the main contributions concerning BMI and DTs in incumbent companies.

All in all, from the review of the literature, a strong link between DTs and BMI emerges. The extant studies have investigated this relationship using different perspectives, including the relationships between business models, technological innovation, and entrepreneurship, the intersection of BMI and technological disruption, the impact of the IIoT on business models, and BMI in SMEs in the context of Industry 4.0.

Regarding the research stream on BMI and DTs in established companies, we analysed it through the lens of what the BM literature generally regards as the three main pillars of BMs, i.e., value creation, value proposition, and value capture. From our review, it emerges that DTs add value by improving operational efficiency, facilitating real-time data sharing in the supply chain, and enabling informed decision-making. However, value creation can be hindered by the presence of cognitive barriers, and could lead to issues related to labour market dynamics. The value proposition is changing through data mining and analytics, leading to innovative offerings and customization, and improving the company's ability to meet changing consumer demands. Therefore, DTs enable incumbents to effectively address new market demands, manage change, and offer highly customized and high-quality products. We also see that DTs enhance value capture through better interconnectivity between companies, greater customer reach, and increased customer engagement. Finally, we can posit that traditional BMs can continue to coexist with new models supported by DTs, but strategic adaptation is required to maintain competitiveness. In this context, personalized and customer-designed products play a more important role, and DTs are critical to helping companies engage with new markets and customers.

This chapter thus offers a compact but detailed account of a topic that is gaining increasing importance and can provide a useful roadmap to researchers who are interested in this subject, especially those who are not very accustomed to this strand of literature. Despite that, we recognize that there are some potential critical issues. The first one concerns the criteria and keywords used to extract the dataset: these keywords come from a thorough *a priori* analysis of the literature and are expected to be suitable for investigating the selected topic. However, the choice of a different set of keywords or the criteria to classify the literature could have resulted in a partially different dataset. In addition, it is possible to extend the analysis to other data providers, such as Web of Science or Google Scholar. Finally, a more exhaustive review may include not only published articles, but also working papers, non-academic media, industry reports and conference proceedings.

REFERENCES

Amit R., Zott C. (2001). Value creation in e-business. *Strategic Management Journal*, 22(6–7), pp. 493–520. https://doi.org/10.1002/smj.187.

Anwar M., Shah S.A. (2018). Managerial networking and business model innovation: Empirical study of new ventures in an emerging economy. *Journal of Small Business and Entrepreneurship*, 32(3), pp. 265–286. https://doi.org//10.1080/08276331.2018.1490509.

Aspara J., Lamberg J.A., Laukia A., Tikkanen H. (2013). Corporate business model transformation and inter-organizational cognition: The case of Nokia. *Long Range Planning*, 46(6), pp. 459–474. https://doi.org/10.1016/j.lrp.2011.06.001.

Baden-Fuller C., Haefliger S. (2013). Business models and technological innovation. *Long Range Planning*, 46(6), pp. 419–426. https://doi.org//10.1016/j.lrp.2013.08.023.

Barney J. (1991). Firm resources and sustained competitive advantage. *Journal of Management*, 17(1), pp. 99–120. https://doi.org//10.1016/S0742-3322(00)17018-4.

Baumol W.J. (2004). Entrepreneurial enterprises, large established firms and other components of the free-market growth machine. *Small Business Economics*, 23(1), pp. 9–21. https://www.jstor.org/stable/40229341.

Berends H., Smits A., Reymen I., Podoynitsyna K. (2016). Learning while (re) configuring: Business model innovation processes in established firms. *Strategic Organization*, 14(3), pp. 181–219. https://doi.org/10.1177/1476127016632758.

Berman S.J. (2012). Digital transformation: Opportunities to create new business models. *Strategy and Leadership*. 40(2), pp. 16–24. https:// doi .org/ 10 .1108/ 10878571211209314.

Bogers M., Hadar R., Bilberg A. (2016). Additive manufacturing for consumer-centric business models: Implications for supply chains in consumer goods manufacturing. *Technological Forecasting and Social Change*, 102, pp. 225–239. https://doi.org/10 .1016/j.techfore.2015.07.024.

Bollweg L., Lackes R., Siepermann M., Weber P. (2019). Drivers and barriers of the digitalisation of local owner operated retail outlets. *Journal of Small Business and Entrepreneurship*, 32(2), pp. 173–201. https://doi.org//10.1080/08276331.2019 .1616256.

Bowman H., Nikou S., de Reuver M. (2019). Digitalization, business models, and SMEs: How do business model innovation practices improve performance of digitalising SMEs?. *Telecommunications Policy*, 43, No. 101828. https://doi.org//10.1016/ j.telpol.2019.101828.

Brenk S., Lüttgens D., Diener K., Piller F. (2019). Learning from failures in business model innovation: Solving decision-making logic conflicts through intrapreneurial effectuation. *Journal of Business Economics*, 89(8), pp. 1097–1147. https://doi.org/ 10.1007/s11573-019-00954-1.

Bresciani S., Ferraris A., Del Giudice M. (2018). The management of organizational ambidexterity through alliances in a new context of analysis: Internet of Things (IoT) smart city projects. *Technological Forecasting and Social Change*, 136, pp. 331–338, https://doi.org/10.1016/j.techfore.2017.03.002.

Brock K., den Ouden E., van der Klauw K., Podoynitsyna K., Langerak F. (2019). Light the way for smart cities: Lessons from Philips lighting. *Technological Forecasting and Social Change*, 142, pp. 194–209. https:// doi .org/ 10.1016/j .techfore .2018.07 .021.

Brown J.R., Fazzari S.M., Petersen B.C. (2009). Financing innovation and growth: Cash flow, external equity, and the 1990s R&D boom. *Journal of Finance*, 64, pp. 151–185. https://doi.org/10.1111/j.1540-6261.2008.01431.x.

Bucherer E., Eisert U., Gassmann O. (2012). Towards systematic business model innovation: Lessons from product innovation management. *Creativity and Innovation Management*, 21(2), pp. 183–198. https://doi.org/10.1108/10878571211242920.

Caputo A., Marzi G., Pellegrini M.M. (2016). The Internet of Things in manufacturing innovation processes: Development and application of a conceptual framework. *Business Process Management Journal*, 22(2). https:// doi .org/ 10 .1108/ BPMJ -05 -2015-0072.

Casadesus-Masanell R., Zhu F. (2013). Business model innovation and competitive imitation: The case of sponsor-based business models. *Strategic Management Journal*, 34(4), pp. 464–482. https://doi.org/10.1002/smj.2022.

Casadesus-Masanell R., Ricart J.E. (2010). How to design a winning business model. *Long Range Planning*, 43(2–3), pp. 195–215. https://doi.org/10.1016/j.lrp.2010.01 .004.

Chesbrough H. (2010). Business model innovation: Opportunities and barriers. *Long Range Planning*, 43(2–3), pp. 354–363. https://doi.org//10.1016/j.lrp.2009.07.010.

Chesbrough H., Rosenbloom R.S. (2002). The role of the business model in capturing value from innovation: Evidence from Xerox Corporation's technology spin-off companies. *Industrial and Corporate Change*, 11(3), pp. 529–555. https://doi.org/10.1093/icc/11.3.529.

Christensen C.M., Bartman T., Van Bever D. (2016). The hard truth about business model innovation. *MIT Sloan Management Review*, 58(1), pp. 31–40.

Ciulli F., Kolk A. (2019). Incumbents and business model innovation for the sharing economy: Implications for sustainability. *Journal of Cleaner Production*, 214, pp. 995–1010. https://doi.org//10.1016/j.jclepro.2018.12.295.

Cliffe S., McGrath R.G. (2011). When your business model is in trouble. *Harvard Business Review*, 89(1–2), pp. 96–98.

Coad A., Rao R. (2008). Innovation and firm growth in high-tech sectors: A quantile regression approach, *Research Policy*, 37(4), pp. 633–648. https://doi.org/10.1016/j.respol.2008.01.003.

Cortimiglia M.N., Ghezzi A., Frank, A.G. (2016). Business model innovation and strategy making nexus: Evidence from a cross-industry mixed-methods study. *R&D Management*, 46(3), pp. 414–432. https://doi.org/10.1111/radm.12113.

Cozzolino A., Verona G., Rothaermel F.T., (2018). Unpacking the disruption process: New technology, business models, and incumbent adaptation. *Journal of Management Studies*, 55(7), pp. 1166–1202. https://doi.org/10.1111/joms.12352.

Cozzolino A., Corbo L., Aversa P. (2021). Digital platform-based ecosystems: The evolution of collaboration and competition between incumbent producers and entrant platforms. *Journal of Business Research*, 126, pp. 385–400. https://doi.org/10.1016/j.jbusres.2020.12.058.

Cucculelli, M., Bettinelli, C. (2015). Business models, intangibles and firm performance: Evidence on corporate entrepreneurship from Italian manufacturing SMEs. *Small Business Economics* 45, pp. 329–350. https://doi.org/10.1007/s11187-015-9631-7.

Cucculelli, M., Peruzzi, V. (2020). Post-crisis firm survival, business model changes, and learning: Evidence from the Italian manufacturing industry. *Small Business Economics* 54, pp. 459–474. https://doi.org/10.1007/s11187-018-0044-2.

Demil B., Lecocq X. (2010). Business model evolution: In search of dynamic consistency. *Long Range Planning*, 43(2–3), pp. 227–246. https://doi.org/10.1016/j.lrp.2010.02.004.

Dijkman R.M., Sprenkels B., Peeters T., Janssen A. (2015). Business models for the internet of things. *International Journal Information Management*, 35(6), pp. 672–678. https://doi.org/10.1016/j. ijinfomgt.2015.07.008.

D'Ippolito B., Messeni Petruzzelli A., Panniello U. (2019). Archetypes of incumbents' strategic responses to digital innovation. *Journal of Intellectual Capital*, 20(5), pp. 662–679. https://doi.org/10.1108/JIC-04-2019-0065.

Egfjord K.F.H., Sund K.J. (2020). Do you see what I see? How differing perceptions of the environment can hinder radical business model innovation. *Technological Forecasting and Social Change*, 150, No. 119787. https://doi.org/10.1016/j.techfore.2019.119787.

Fakhar Manesh M., Pellegrini M.M., Marzi G., Dabi'c M. (2020). Knowledge management in the fourth industrial revolution: Mapping the literature and scoping future avenues. *IEEE Transactions on Engineering Management*, 68(1).

FitzGerald E., Ferguson R., Adams A., Gaved M., Mor Y., Thomas R. (2013). Augmented reality and mobile learning: The state of the art. *International Journal Mobile Blended Learning*, 5(4), pp. 43–58. https://doi.org/10.4018/ijmbl.2013100103.

Foss N.J., Saebi T. (2018). Business models and business model innovation: Between wicked and paradigmatic problems. *Long Range Planning*, 51(1), pp. 9–21. https://doi.org//10.1016/j.lrp.2017.07.006.

Foss N.J., Saebi T. (2017). Fifteen years of research on business model innovation: How far have we come, and where should we go?. *Journal of Management*, 43(1), pp. 200–227. https://doi.org/10.1177/0149206316675927.

Foss N.J., Saebi T. (Eds.). (2015). *Business Model Innovation: The Organisational Dimension*. Oxford: OUP Oxford.

Frank A.G., Dalenogare L.S., Ayala N.F. (2019). Industry 4.0 technologies: Implementation patterns in manufacturing companies. *International Journal of Production Economics*, 210, pp. 15–26. https://doi.org/10.1016/j.ijpe.2019.01.004.

Frankenberger K., Weiblen T., Csik M., Gassmann O. (2013). The 4I-framework of business model innovation: A structured view on process phases and challenges. *International Journal of Product Development*, 18(3–4), pp. 249–273. https://doi.org/10.1504/IJPD.2013.055012.

Gassmann O., Frankenberger K., Csik M. (2014). *The Business Model Navigator: 55 Models That Will Revolutionise Your Business*. London: Pearson UK.

Geels F.W., Kern F., Fuchs G., Hinderer N., Gregor Kungl G., Mylan J., Neukirch M., Wassermann S. (2016). The enactment of socio-technical transition pathways: A reformulated typology and a comparative multi-level analysis of the German and UK low-carbon electricity transitions (1990–2014). *Research Policy*, 45(4), pp. 896–913, ISSN 0048-7333, https://doi.org/10.1016/j.respol.2016.01.015.

Gerstner W.-C., König A., Enders A., Hambrick D.C. (2013). CEO narcissism, audience engagement, and organizational adoption of technological discontinuities. *Administrative Science Quarterly*, 58(2), pp. 257–291. https://doi.org/10.1177/0001839213488773.

Grigoriou K., Rothaermel F.T. (2017). Organizing for knowledge generation: Internal knowledge networks and the contingent effect of external knowledge sourcing. *Strategic Management Journal*, 38(2), 395–414. https://doi.org/10.1002/smj.2489.

Gruber H., Koutroumpis P. (2013). Competition enhancing regulation and diffusion of innovation: The case of broadband networks. *Journal of Regulatory Economics*, 43, pp. 168–195. https://doi.org/10.1007/s11149-012-9205-4.

Habtay S.R., Holmén M. (2014). Incumbents' responses to disruptive business model innovation: The moderating role of technology vs market-driven innovation. *International Journal of Entrepreneurship and Innovation Management*, 18(4), pp. 289–309. https://doi.org//10.1504/IJEIM.2014.064211.

Haftor D.M., Costa R.C., 2023. Five dimensions of business model innovation: A multi-case exploration of industrial incumbent firm's business model transformations, *Journal of Business Research*, Volume 154, 113352, ISSN 0148-2963, https://doi.org/10.1016/j.jbusres.2022.113352.

Hänninen M., Smedlund A., Mitronen L. (2018). Digitalization in retailing: Multi-sided platforms as drivers of industry transformation. *Baltic Journal of Management*, 13(2), pp. 152–168. https://doi.org/10.1108/BJM-04-2017-0109.

Hinings B., Gegenhuber T., Greenwood R. (2018). Digital innovation and transformation: An institutional perspective. *Information and Organization*, 28(1), pp. 52–61. https://doi.org/10.1016/j.infoandorg.2018.02.004.

Ibarra D., Ganzarain J., Igartua J.I. (2018). Business model innovation through Industry 4.0: A review. *Procedia Manufacturing*, 22, pp. 4–10. https://doi.org//10.1016/j.promfg.2018.03.002.

Johnson M.W., Christensen C.M., Kagermann H. (2008). Reinventing your business model. *Harvard Business Review*, 86(12), pp. 57–68.

Kenney M., Zysman J. (2019) The platform economy: Restructuring the space of capitalist accumulation. *Cambridge Journal of Regions, Economy and Society*, 13(1), pp. 55–76. https://doi.org/10.1093/cjres/rsaa001.

Khanagha S., Volberda H., Oshri I. (2014). Business model renewal and ambidexterity: Structural alteration and strategy formation process during transition to a cloud business model. *R&D Management*, 44(January 2013), pp. 322–340. https://doi.org//10.1111/radm.12070.

Khanagha S., Ansari S.S., Paroutis S., Oviedo L. (2022). Mutualism and the dynamics of new platform creation: A study of Cisco and fog computing. *Strategic Management Journal*, 43(3), pp. 476–506. https://doi.org/10.1002/smj.3147.

Kiel D., Arnold C., Voigt, K.I. (2017). The influence of the Industrial Internet of Things on business models of established manufacturing companies – A business level perspective. *Technovation*, 68, pp. 4–19. https://doi.org//10.1016/j.technovation.2017.09.003.

Kim S.K., Min S. (2015). Business model innovation performance: When does adding a new business model benefit an incumbent? *Strategic Entrepreneurship Journal*, 9(1), pp. 34–57. https://doi.org/10.1002/sej.1193.

Klos C., Spieth P., Clauss T., Klusmann C. (2021). Digital transformation of incumbent firms: A business model innovation perspective. *IEEE Transactions on Engineering Management*, 70(6), pp. 2017–2033. https://doi.org/10.1109/TEM.2021.3075502.

Kohtamäki M., Parida V., Oghazi P., Gebauer H., Baines T. (2019). Digital servitization business models in ecosystems: A theory of the firm. *Journal of Business Research*, 104, pp. 380–392. https://doi.org/10.1016/j.jbusres.2019.06.027.

Kotarba M. (2018). Digital transformation of business models. *Foundation of Management*, 10(1), pp. 123–142. https://doi.org/10.2478/fman-2018-0011.

Kumar R., Singh R.K., Dwivedi Y.K. (2020). Application of industry 4.0 technologies in SMEs for ethical and sustainable operations: Analysis of challenges. *Journal of Cleaner Production*, 275, 124063. https://doi.org/10.1016/j.jclepro.2020.124063.

Latilla V.M.M., Urbinati A., Cavallo A. (2021). Organizational re-design for business model innovation while exploiting digital technologies: A single case study of an energy company. *International Journal of Innovation and Technology Management*, 18(2). https://doi.org/10.1142/S0219877020400027.

Li F. (2018). The digital transformation of business models in the creative industries: A holistic framework and emerging trends. *Technovation*, 92–93, No. 102012. https://doi.org/10.1016/j.technovation.2017.12.004.

Libert B., Beck M., Wind Y.J. (2016). 7 Questions to ask before your next digital transformation. *Harvard Business Review*, 60(12), pp. 11–13.

Liu P., Bell R. (2019). Exploration of the initiation and process of business model innovation of successful Chinese ICT enterprises. *Journal of Entrepreneurship in Emerging Economies*, 11(4), pp. 515–536. https://doi.org//10.1108/JEEE-09-2018-0094.

Markides C. (2006). Disruptive innovation: In need of better theory. *Journal of Product Innovation Management*, 23(1), pp. 19–25. https://doi.org/10.1111/j.1540-5885.2005.00177.x.

Markides C., Charitou C.D. (2004). Competing with dual business models: A contingency approach. *Academy of Management Perspectives*, 18(3), pp. 22–36. https://doi.org//10.5465/ame.2004.14776164.

McGrath, R., McManus, R. (2020). Discovery-driven planning. *Harvard Business Review.*

Metallo C., Agrifoglio R., Schiavone F., Muelle, J. (2018). Understanding business model in the internet of things industry. *Technological Forecasting and Social Change.* 136, pp. 298–306. https://doi.org/10.1016/j.techfore.2018.01.020.

Moeuf A., Pellerin R., Lamouri S., Tamayo-Giraldo S., Barbaray R. (2018). The industrial management of SMEs in the era of Industry 4.0. *International Journal of Production Research*, 56(3), pp. 1118–1136. https://doi.org//10.1080/00207543 .2017.1372647.

Müller J.M., Buliga O., Voigt K.I. (2018). Fortune favors the prepared: How SMEs approach business model innovation in Industry 4.0. *Technological Forecasting and Social Change*, 132, pp. 2–17. https://doi.org//10.1016/j.techfore.2017.12.019.

Nagy J., Oláh J., Erdei E., Máté D., Popp J. (2018). The role and impact of industry 4.0 and the internet of things on the business strategy of the value chain—The case of Hungary. *Sustainability*, 10(10), No. 3491. https://doi.org//10.3390/su10103491.

Nambisan S. (2017). Digital entrepreneurship: Toward a digital technology perspective of entrepreneurship. *Entrepreneurship Theory and Practice*, 41(6), pp. 1029–1055. https://doi.org//10.1111/etap.12254.

Nambisan S., Wright M., Feldman M. (2018). The digital transformation of innovation and entrepreneurship: Progress, challenges and key themes, *Research Policy*, 48(8), https://doi.org/10.1016/j.respol.2019.03.018.

Osiyevskyy O., Dewald, J. (2015a). Inducements, impediments, and immediacy: Exploring the cognitive drivers of small business managers' intentions to adopt business model change. *Journal of Small Business Management*, 53(4), pp. 1011–1032. https://doi.org//10.1111/jsbm.12113.

Osiyevskyy O., Dewald, J. (2015b). Explorative versus exploitative business model change: The cognitive antecedents of firm-level responses to disruptive innovation. *Strategic Entrepreneurship Journal*, 9(1), pp. 58–78. https://doi.org/10.1002/sej .1192.

Osterwalder A., Pigneur Y., Tucci C.L. (2005). Clarifying business models: Origins, present, and future of the concept. *Communications of the Association for Information Systems*, 16(1), 1. https://doi.org//10.17705/1CAIS.01601.

Osterwalder A., Pigneur Y. (2010). *Business Model Generation: A Handbook for Visionaries, Game Changers, and Challengers.* Hoboken: John Wiley and Sons.

Pateli A.G., Giaglis G.M. (2005). Technology innovation-induced business model change: A contingency approach. *Journal of Organizational Change Management*, 18(2), pp. 167–183.

Rachinger M., Rauter R., Müller C., Vorraber W., Schirgi E. (2019). Digitalization and its influence on business model innovation. *Journal of Manufacturing Technology Management*, 30(8), pp. 1143–1160. https://doi.org//10.1108/JMTM-01-2018-0020.

Saebi T., Lien L., Foss N.J. (2017). What drives business model adaptation? The impact of opportunities, threats and strategic orientation. *Long Range Planning*, 50(5), pp. 567–581. https://doi.org/10.1016/j.lrp.2016.06.006.

Santos J., Spector B., der Heyden L. Van. (2009). Toward a theory of business model innovation within incumbent firms. *INSEAD*, Fontainebleau, France, pp. 1–53. https://doi.org/10.2139/ssrn.1362515.

Schallmo D., Williams C.A., Boardman L. (2017). Digital transformation of business models—Best practice, enablers, and roadmap. *International Journal Innovation Management*, 21(08), 1740014. https://doi.org/10.1142/S136391961740014X.

Schneider S., Spieth P. (2013). Business model innovation: Towards an integrated future research agenda. *International Journal of Innovation Management*, 17(01), 1340001. https://doi.org/10.1142/ S136391961340001X.

Sorenson R.L. (2000). The contribution of leadership style and practices to family and business success. *Family Business Review*, 13(3), pp. 183–200. https:// doi.org/ 10 .1111/j.1741-6248.2000.00183.x.

Sorescu A., Frambach R.T., Singh J., Rangaswamy A., Bridges C. (2011). Innovations in retail business models. *Journal of Retailing*, 87(1), pp. 3–16. https://doi.org/10 .1016/j.jretai.2011.04.005.

Sosna M., Trevinyo-Rodriguez R.N., Velamuri S.R. (2010). Business model innovation through trial-and-error learning: The Naturhouse case. *Long Range Planning*, 43, pp. 383–407. https://doi.org/10.1016/j.lrp.2010.02.003.

Sund K.J., Bogers M.L., Sahramaa M. (2021). Managing business model exploration in incumbent firms: A case study of innovation labs in European banks. *Journal of Business Research*, 128, pp. 11–19. https://doi.org/10.1016/j.jbusres.2021.01.059.

Taran Y., Boer H., Lindgren P. (2015). A business model innovation typology. *Decision Sciences*, 46(2), pp. 301–331. https://doi.org/10.1111/deci.12128.

Teece D.J. (2010). Business models, business strategy and innovation. *Long Range Planning*, 43(2–3), pp. 172–194. https://doi.org/10.1016/j.lrp.2009.07.003.

Tilson D., Lyytinen K., Sørensen C. (2010). Research commentary—digital infra-structures: The missing IS research agenda. *Information System Research*, 21(4), pp. 748–759. https://doi.org/10.1287/isre.1100.0318.

Tripsas M., Gavetti G. (2000). Capabilities, cognition, and inertia: Evidence from digital imaging. *Strategic Management Journal*, 21(10–11), pp. 1147–1161. https:// doi.org/10.1002/1097-0266(200010/11)21:10/11<1147::AID-SMJ128>3.0.CO;2-R.

Verhoef P.C., Broekhuizen T., Bart Y., Bhattacharya A., Dong J.Q., Fabian N., Haenlein M. (2021). Digital transformation: A multidisciplinary reflection and research agenda. *Journal of Business Research*, 122(889), pp. 901. https://doi.org/10 .1016/j.jbusres.2019.09.022.

Vial G. (2019). Understanding digital transformation: A review and a research agenda. *Journal of Strategic Information Systems*, 28(2), pp. 118–144. https:// doi .org/ 10 .1016/j.jsis.2019.01.003.

Volberda H.W., Khanagha S., Baden-Fuller C., Mihalache O.R., Birkinshaw J. (2021). Strategizing in a digital world: Overcoming cognitive barriers, reconfiguring routines and introducing new organizational forms. *Long Range Planning*, 54(5), https://doi.org/10.1016/j.lrp.2021.102110.

Warner K.S., Wäger M. (2019). Building dynamic capabilities for digital transfor-mation: An ongoing process of strategic renewal. *Long Range Planning*, 52(3), pp. 326–349. https://doi.org/10.1016/j.lrp.2018.12.001.

Yeager D., Shenhar A. (2019). A unified framework for business model transformation of established firms. *Journal of Business Models*, 7(4), pp. 73–78. https://doi.org/10 .5278/ojs.jbm.v7i4.3134.

Yoo Y., Henfridsson O., Lyytinen K. (2010). Research commentary: The new organ-izing logic of digital innovation: An agenda for information systems research. *Information System Research*, 21(4), pp. 724–735. https:// www .jstor .org/ stable/ 23015640.

Zaki M. (2019). Digital transformation: Harnessing digital technologies for the next generation of services. *Journal of Services Marketing*, 33(4), pp. 429–435. http://dx .doi.org/10.1108/JSM-01-2019-0034.

Zott C., Amit R. (2007). Business model design and the performance of entrepreneur-
    ial firms. *Organization Science*, 18(2), pp. 181–199. https://www.jstor.org/stable/
    25146093.
Zott C., Amit R. (2013). The business model: A theoretically anchored robust construct
    for strategic analysis. *Strategic Organization*, 11(4), pp. 403–411. https://doi.org/10
    .1177/ 1476127013510466.

2. Business model innovation and the adoption of digital technologies in incumbent firms

Riccardo Cappelli, Jasmine Mondolo and Marco Cucculelli

1. INTRODUCTION

The last 15 years or so have been marked by an unprecedented wave of technological change, which has been affecting an increasing number of sectors – including 'traditional' sectors, such as agriculture – and countries. The ongoing digital transformation has a relevant but ambiguous impact on workers, companies and societies. On the one hand, it challenges established sectors, which may lag behind and may not be able to cope with this dynamic and competitive environment, and can negatively affect the economy or the society (e.g., Shen et al., 2018; Brynjolfsson & McAfee, 2014; Frey & Osborne, 2017). For instance, a large body of literature on the effects of technological change on employment has shown that new technologies, especially automation technologies, can replace some tasks that were previously performed by workers, especially routine tasks (see Sebastian & Biagi, 2018, for a review of the literature on the so-called 'routine-biased technological change hypothesis'). On the other hand, the latest wave of technological progress also creates opportunities. This particularly holds for dynamic companies adopting digital technologies and hiring workers with digital skills, which often experience benefits in terms of productivity, firm performance and even employment compared to non-adopters (e.g., Acemoglu et al., 2020; Domini et al., 2021; Koch, Manuylov & Smolka, 2021). Entrepreneurs who intend to reap the benefits of the technological revolution leverage these digital technologies to finance and carry out further innovation (Ahrens et al., 2019; Audretsch et al., 2016), create new digital products and services, and innovate their business models (BMs). As far as BMs are concerned, they are not something static and immutable; in fact, they tend to change over time, and in doing so, they help firms stay competitive and keep up with a dynamic and rapidly evolving scenario.

One of the factors that may facilitate the emergence of new business models is the introduction of advanced technologies. As highlighted by Baden-Fuller & Haefliger (2013, p.424), 'The business model may have to change in order to appropriate features of a technology that create customer value. Also, elements of the model may change in order to allow technology to be developed that fits customer needs or that emerges from the customer directly.' A broad strand of literature has tackled the link between digitalization, digital technologies or skills and business model innovation (BMI), and suggests that the former significantly affect BM diversity and directly or indirectly spur BMI (see Section 2). However, empirical evidence on the role of the adoption of digital technologies in business model changes is still scant, and this is probably mainly attributable to limited data availability. In particular, business models rest on a quite broad and elusive concept, which makes it difficult to find adequate measures.

In light of these considerations, in this chapter we attempt to advance our knowledge on the role of digital technologies in business model reconfiguration – i.e., in business model innovation carried out in incumbent firms. To this end, we exploit first-hand, firm-level information from a survey that we administered to about 6,000 Italian incumbent companies at the end of 2019. This extensive survey, which covers several relevant aspects of a business, also comprises a set of questions aimed to collect information on the changes that occurred during a previous period in different types of business activities. Moreover, the surveyed companies are asked whether they have adopted at least one of the ten advanced digital technologies identified. The regression analysis reveals that the intensity of technology adoption is positively associated with the intensity of business model change, and that this positive link still holds when the sample is split into two sub-samples according to the firms' sector (i.e., manufacturing and services).

The balance of this study is organized as follows. Section 2 shortly reviews the pertinent literature. Section 3 presents the empirical strategy. Section 4 illustrates the results of the regression analysis. Section 5 concludes.

2.   LITERATURE REVIEW

A sizable and heterogeneous strand of literature has jointly analysed the link between digital technologies and BMI. For instance, some articles analyse different categorizations of digital-driven BMI (e.g., Bellini et al., 2019; Chasin et al., 2020; Li, 2020), while others mainly aim to identify and describe the various phases of the digital-driven BM processes (e.g., Najmaei, 2016; Latilla et al., 2021; Sund et al., 2021). Importantly, some contributions scrutinize the effect of the adoption of digital technologies on BMI. To give some examples, Garzella et al. (2021), who mainly aim to investigate the digital-era role of boundary management capabilities in the processes of BMI in SMEs, assume and then test through Structural Equation Modeling (SEM) applied to survey data on 250 Italian experts that digitalization positively affects boundary size, which in turn fosters BMI. Bouwman et al. (2018) focus on 338 European SMEs actively using social media and Big Data to innovate their BM and, through SEM, show that digitalization/innovation is one of the main drivers of BMI, which in turn positively impacts innovativeness and firm performance. Additionally, a few studies examine the direct or indirect implications of internal digital-related capabilities; for instance, Ciampi et al. (2021) focus on Big Data Analytics Capabilities and apply both PLS-SEM and fuzzy-set Qualitative Comparative Analysis methods to survey data from 253 UK firms to show that Big Data Analytics Capabilities have both direct and indirect positive effects on BMI, with the latter being mediated by entrepreneurial orientation. In a similar vein, Mihardjo et al. (2018, 2019) investigate the contribution of digital skills and orientation to BMI in two samples of tele-communication companies in Indonesia using survey data and Smart-PLS. In particular, Mihardjo et al. (2018) show that distinctive organization capability capturing digital leadership, digital culture and digital agility has a positive influence on BMI which is mediated by co-creation strategy, while Mihardjo and co-authors' study published in 2019 reveals that digital leadership has both direct and indirect effects on customer experience orientation in developing BMI.

To sum up, in recent years, a broad and heterogeneous strand of literature has empirically investigated the relationship between digital technologies or skills and business model innovation; all in all, it reveals that the ongoing digital transformation has significantly impacted BMs, for instance by giving rise to new BM types, by affecting the main components of BMs and by spur-ring BMI. However, there is still limited empirical evidence on the role played by digital technologies as antecedents of business model innovation, and the few existing studies mostly resort to PLS and SEM techniques, use relatively small samples and employ quite broad indicators of digitalization.

3.   EMPIRICAL STRATEGY

3.1   Data

In this study, we mainly rely on information collected from our survey, which we administered to a representative sample of Italian firms with the purpose of shedding light on valuable but hardly measurable corporate aspects. In particu-lar, we ask a number of questions on the adoption of several advanced digital technologies, and, in another section of the questionnaire, we investigate if and how the surveyed companies have recently modified certain important business model components – for instance, if they have introduced new products or processes, if they have modified their pricing policies, or if they have hired new employees with advanced technological skills. More information on the survey is provided in the Appendix.

We match the survey-based information with financial data (e.g., number of employees and Return on Sales (ROS)) from the Bureau van Dijk – Aida database. The final sample, which we obtain after some data cleaning, and in particular after removing the observations for which some information on the selected variables is not available, consists of 2,514 Italian incumbent firms operating in manufacturing or service sectors. In the next section, we provide a short description of the dependent variable, the key regressor and the control variables.

3.2   Variables

3.2.1   Dependent variable

In line with the existing literature, we identify business model innovation by analysing the changes in the activities performed in several functional areas (Lanzolla & Markides, 2021). Specifically, the dependent variable is *Business model innovation*, which measures the intensity of the changes that previously occurred in four main types of business activities, i.e., product and process activities, financial activities, organizational activities, and external relational activities. The information used to build this variable comes from 28 questions of the survey covering the aforementioned areas. To give some examples, firms are asked: whether they have carried out new product or process innovation (product and process activities); whether they have adopted new selling methods (e.g., pay-per-use or licensing) and new pricing strategies (financial activities); whether they have introduced a new business function or hired people with new skills (organizational activities); whether they have modified or introduced new sales channels or whether activities up and down the supply chain have been integrated (external relational activities). To create our dependent variable, we sum up all the adjustments indicated by the surveyed firms in each of the four functional areas. Finally, we divide the absolute value of this variable by 28 – i.e., the number of all the possible BM changes considered – in order for it to range between 0 and 1.

Table 2.1 shows the mean number of changes by business model area and their pairwise correlations. We see that the organizational area displays the highest average amount of changes (2.2), followed by the product (2.1), finance (1.8), and networking/relational (1.7) areas, and that the sampled companies have recently implemented, on average, about eight changes concerning

Table 2.1   *Mean number of business model changes by functional area and their pairwise correlations*

	Business area	Number of changes	(1)	(2)	(3)	(4)	(5)
(1)	Product area	2.1	1				
(2)	Organizational area	2.2	0.5	1			
(3)	Networking area	1.7	0.5	0.5	1		
(4)	Financial area	1.8	0.5	0.4	0.5	1	
(5)	Total	7.9	0.8	0.8	0.8	0.7	1

Source: Authors' elaboration based on our survey data.

various business aspects. Finally, we can notice that the different BM changes are positively correlated, and that the pairwise correlations range between 0.4 and 0.5.

3.2.2   Key regressor

The key regressor of our empirical analysis, labelled *Technology adoption index*, measures the extent of the firms' adoption of different (categories of) advanced digital technologies ('IoT, Big data, Industry Analytics', 'Additive manufacturing', 'Augmented Reality', 'Wearable devices', 'Business Intelligence and CRM', 'Cloud Computing', 'Collaborative robots', 'Cyber security', 'Interconnected machinery', 'Management systems'). As in the case of *business model innovation*, we divide the absolute value of this variable by ten – i.e., the number of all the categories of digital technologies covered by the survey – in order to make it range between 0 and 1.

Table 2.2 shows the adoption rates of the selected technologies across firms. We observe that almost 60.6 per cent of the sampled companies have adopted none of the advanced digital technologies considered, and that only five out of almost 2,500 firms have implemented all of them. This suggests that, although several Italian businesses have recently undertaken processes of digitalization, a significant number of companies still lag behind.

Figure 2.1 displays, for each of the ten technologies under scrutiny, the percentage of adopters in our sample. We can see that cyber security systems, CRM (Customer Relationship Management) and the IoT (Internet of Things) have been adopted by at least 10 per cent of the sampled firms; conversely, the widespread of other sophisticated technologies such as augmented reality, additive manufacturing and collaborative robots is more limited.

Finally, Figure 2.2 shows the (average) number of business model changes across various levels of technology adoption. Notably, we observe a positive correlation between the number of adopted technologies and the number of business model changes.

Table 2.2   *Adoption rates of advanced digital technologies across firms*

Number of adopted technologies	Number of firms	Percentage
0	1,523	60.58
1	492	19.57
2	278	11.06
3	108	4.3
4	63	2.51
5	26	1.03
6	9	0.36
7	7	0.28
8	3	0.12
9	0	0
10	5	0.2

Source: Authors' elaboration based on our survey data.

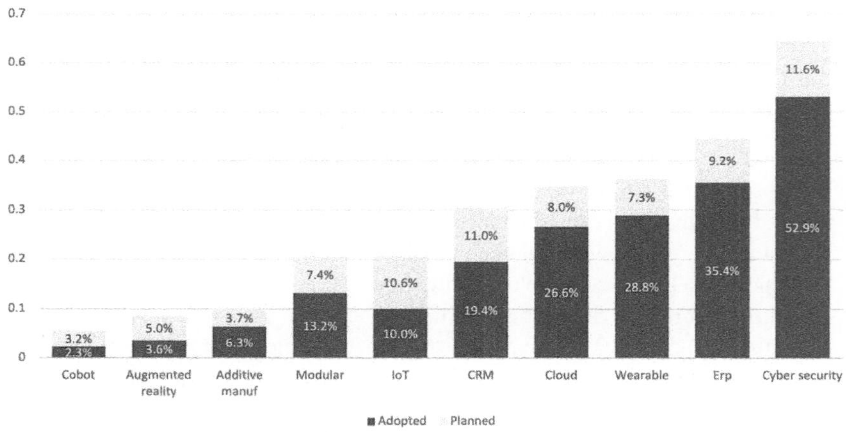

Figure 2.1   *Firm's technology adoption rates by type of digital technology*

Source: Authors' elaboration based on our survey data.

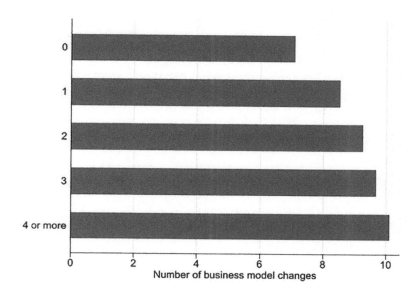

Source: Authors' elaboration based on our survey data.

Figure 2.2   *Number of business model changes (mean values) by intensity of technology adoption*

3.2.3   Control variables

In the regression analysis, we control for some additional factors which might be related to business model innovation. In particular, we consider: the (logarithm) number of employees (*Size*) in 2014; the (logarithm) age of the firm (*Age*); the average ROS measured over the period 2011–2014 (*ROS*); the tenure length (logarithm of the number of years) of the current CEO (*CEO tenure*); the sales' share of the three main customers (*Customer dependence*). Finally, to account for sectoral heterogeneity, we include a set of sectoral dummies (with sectors defined at the NACE Rev.2 3-digit level).

Table 2.3 displays the baseline descriptive statistics of our selected variables. We notice that, on average, the selected companies have implemented about 28 per cent of all the business model changes under scrutiny, and have adopted around 8 per cent of the types of digital technologies considered in the survey. Also, we observe that, on average, these firms are relatively young and small, even though relevant heterogeneity in terms of both firm size and firm age emerges. Finally, we can argue that the mean amount of customer dependence is quite significant, as, on average, almost half of corporate sales are attributable to the three main customers.

Table 2.3   Baseline descriptive statistics (N=2,514)

Variable	Mean	SD	Min	Max
Business model innovation	0.28	0.13	0.14	0.86
Technology adoption index	0.08	0.13	0	1
Age	17.70	13.14	1	95
Size	11.68	16.82	1	650
CEO tenure	16.57	11.28	1	69
ROS	4.52	7.51	-44.13	29.81
Customer dependence	46.10	27.50	1	100

Source: Authors' elaboration based on our survey data and on Aida BvD data.

3.3   Empirical Model

We assess the role played by the adoption of digital technologies and other variables in the firms' reconfiguration of their business model through a regression analysis. Given the ordinal nature of the dependent variable, we run a set of ordinal logistic regressions. First, we perform the estimation on the entire sample, which is made up of 2,514 observations/enterprises. After that, we split the initial sample into two sub-samples according to the sector in which the firms operate, i.e., manufacturing and services, and re-run the ordinal logistic regression for each sub-sample to see whether the link between digital technologies and BMI is affected by sectoral specificities.

4.   RESULTS OF THE REGRESSION ANALYSIS

Table 2.4 reports the results of the ordered logistic regressions for both the total sample (Model 1) and the two previously defined sub-samples (Model 2 and Model 3). We see that our key regressor, the *Technology adoption index*, is positively associated with business model innovation (Model 1). This positive relationship still holds when we separately consider manufacturing companies (Model 2) and service companies (Model 3). These findings support and strengthen the preliminary evidence provided by the existing literature that digital technologies are a driver of business model innovation, which in turn boosts firms' competitiveness and resilience and helps them address the challenges posed by the current uncertain and turbulent scenario.

Regarding the control variables, we observe that *CEO tenure* is positively associated with *Business model innovation*, and that the result for the overall sample (Model 1) is driven by manufacturing companies (Model 2). This suggests that a longer CEO experience, during which he/she has probably

Table 2.4   Determinants of business model innovation

VARIABLES	Model 1	Model 2	Model 3
	Total	Manufacturing	Services
Technology adoption index	3.542***	3.959***	3.261***
	(0.311)	(0.474)	(0.413)
Age	-0.197***	-0.157*	-0.229***
	(0.057)	(0.086)	(0.078)
Size	0.080*	0.093	0.081
	(0.044)	(0.079)	(0.053)
CEO tenure	0.117**	0.158**	0.086
	(0.049)	(0.074)	(0.065)
ROS	-0.002	-0.009	0.001
	(0.005)	(0.009)	(0.006)
Customer sales dependence	-0.176***	-0.298***	-0.119**
	(0.044)	(0.078)	(0.054)
Observations	2,514	1,062	1,452
Log likelihood	-5823.9	-2401.6	-3402.4

Notes: Industry fixed effects are included in all the models; standard errors in parentheses;
*** $p<0.01$, ** $p<0.05$, * $p<0.1$.

run across unpredicted and adverse events, fuels the firm's ability to adjust its business model when faced with a changing environment. Also, *Age* is negatively correlated with business model innovation, i.e., older firms, which may be more prone to inertia than younger and more dynamic businesses, are less likely to adjust their business model. The variable firm size (*Size*) displays a positive and marginally significant coefficient (Model 1) that becomes insignificant in the sub-sample estimates (Models 2 and 3). Conversely, the coefficient of the variable *Customer sales dependence* is negative; hence, a strong dependence on few customers, which generally implies less flexibility and leeway, may become penalizing when the company intends to innovate its business model. Interestingly, the variable *ROS*, which is a widely used accounting indicator of firm performance, is nonsignificant; accordingly, it seems that firms' business model changes are not significantly related to past firm performance.

5.   CONCLUSIONS

The last two decades, and in particular the most recent years, have been marked by increasing globalization and competition, as well as by some significant negative shocks – e.g., the financial crisis in 2009 and the Covid-19 pandemic – which have strengthened the firms' need of performing BMI as a response to such uncertain and turbulent periods. Among the various human and non-human factors that can influence an organization's ability to respond to changes in the competitive arena, the adoption of digital technologies has been increasingly recognized as an important driver of BMI by academics, managers, and policymakers. Despite that, and probably due to the lack of firm-level information on these variables, and to the measurement issues related to business models and BMI, rigorous quantitative evidence that supports the alleged role of digital technologies as antecedents of BMI is still scant.

To fill this gap, using a survey-based dataset covering 2,514 Italian incumbent firms, we empirically test whether the introduction of advanced digital technologies fosters business model innovation. We show that the adoption of these technologies is positively associated with BMI in both the manufacturing and the service sectors. Accordingly, this chapter strengthens the preliminary evidence provided by previous literature (e.g., Bouwman et al., 2018; Ciampi et al., 2021; Garzella et al., 2021).

This finding should motivate companies that are not keeping up with the latest technological wave to invest in new digital technologies, as the related costs and efforts are likely to be more than offset by the benefits associated with business model innovation. Importantly, BM changes, especially in the current uncertain and highly competitive scenario, may become necessary for avoiding strong losses or, in some cases, the end of the business. In light of these results, policymakers should support companies that intend to undertake a process of digitalization, for instance by partly covering the costs for the training of the current personnel and the hiring of new, highly skilled employees.

Our study presents some limitations. First, we assess the role of digital technologies on the overall change in business models; it would be interesting, for example, to separately consider business model elements that are related to the value creation process (e.g., elements concerning the manufacturing processes) vs other elements more pertaining to the value creation process (e.g., aspects related to pricing strategy). Second, we do not test whether the link between digital technologies and business model innovation is moderated by complementary assets, such as the firm's endowment of human capital. Third, we do not address the economic effects of BMI, and in particular we do not know yet, also due to limited data availability and the distortions caused by Covid-19, whether technology-driven business model changes have been resulting in increased economic performance. Future research may address some of the aforementioned issues.

REFERENCES

Acemoglu, D., Lelarge, C., Restrepo, P. (2020). Competing with Robots: Firm-Level Evidence from France. *AEA Papers and Proceedings*, 110: 383–388, DOI: 10.1257/pandp.20201003.

Ahrens, J.-P., Isaak, A. J., Istipliler, B., Steininger, D. M. (2019). The Star Citizen Phenomenon and the 'Ultimate Dream Management' Technique in Crowdfunding. *Proceedings of the 40th International Conference on Information Systems (ICIS)*, Munich, Germany, pp. 1–9.

Audretsch, D. B., Lehmann, E. E., Paleari, S., Vismara, S. (2016). Entrepreneurial finance and technology transfer. *The Journal of Technology Transfer*, 41(1), 1–9.

Baden-Fuller, C., Haefliger, S. (2013). Business models and technological innovation. *Long Range Planning*, 46, 419–426.

Bellini, F., Dulskaia, I., Savastano, M., D'Ascenzo, F. (2019). Business models innovation for sustainable urban mobility in small and medium-sized European cities. *Management & Marketing, Challenges for the Knowledge Society*, 14(3), 266–277.

Bouwman, H., Nikou, S., Molina-Castillo, F. J., de Reuver, M. (2018). The impact of digitalization on business models. *Digital Policy, Regulation and Governance*, 20(2), 105–124.

Brynjolfsson, E., McAfee, A. (2014). *The Second Machine Age: Work, Progress, and Prosperity in a Time of Brilliant Technologies*. W.W. Norton & Company.

Chasin, F., Paukstadt, U., Gollhardt, T., Becker, J. (2020). Smart energy driven business model innovation: An analysis of existing business models and implications for business model change in the energy sector. *Journal of Cleaner Production*, 269, 122083.

Ciampi, F., Demi, S., Magrini, A., Marzi, G., Papa, A. (2021). Exploring the impact of big data analytics capabilities on business model innovation: The mediating role of entrepreneurial orientation. *Journal of Business Research*, 123, 1–13.

Domini, G., Grazzi, M., Moschella, D., Treibich, T. (2021). Threats and opportunities in the digital era: Automation spikes and employment dynamics. *Research Policy*, 50(7), 104137.

Frey, C. B., Osborne, M. A. (2017). The future of employment: How susceptible are jobs to computerisation? *Technological Forecasting & Social Change*, 114, 254–280.

Garzella, S., Fiorentino, R., Caputo, A., Lardo, A. (2021). Business model innovation in SMEs: The role of boundaries in the digital era. *Technology Analysis & Strategic Management*, 33(1), 31–43.

Koch, M., Manuylov, I., Smolka, M. (2021). Robots and firms. *The Economic Journal*, 131(638), 2553–2584.

Lanzolla, G., Markides, C. (2021), A business model view of strategy. *Journal of Management Studies*, 58(2), 540–553.

Latilla, V. M. M., Urbinati, A., Cavallo, A., Franzò, S., Ghezzi, A. (2021). Organizational redesign for business model innovation while exploiting digital technologies: A single case study of an energy company. *International Journal of Innovation and Technology Management*, 18(2), 2040002.

Li, F. (2020). The digital transformation of business models in the creative industries: A holistic framework and emerging trends. *Technovation*, 92, 102012.

Mihardjo, L. W., Sasmoko, S., Alamsjah, F., Elidjen, E. (2018). The role of distinctive organisational capability in formulating co-creation strategy and business model innovation. *Polish Journal of Management Studies*, 18(2), 197–208.

Mihardjo, L. W., Sasmoko, S., Alamsjah, F., Elidjen, E. (2019). Digital leadership role in developing business model innovation and customer experience orientation in industry 4.0. *Management Science Letters*, 9(11), 1749–1762.

Najmaei, A. (2016). How do entrepreneurs develop business models in small high-tech ventures? An exploratory model from Australian IT firms. *Entrepreneurship Research Journal*, 6(3), 297–343.

Sebastian, R., Biagi, F. (2018). The routine biased technical change hypothesis: A critical review. JRC Working Paper No. 113174, Joint Research Centre (Seville site).

Shen, K. N., Lindsay, V., Xu, Y. (2018). Digital entrepreneurship. *Information Systems Journal*, 28(6), 1125–1128.

Sund, K. J., Bogers, M. L., Sahramaa, M. (2021). Managing business model exploration in incumbent firms: A case study of innovation labs in European banks. *Journal of Business Research*, 128, 11–19.

3. Capturing value along the value chain: the role of business model innovation and technological innovation

Damiano Meloni[1] and Marco Cucculelli

1. INTRODUCTION

In the current competitive and globalized context, a product or service results from a series of stages involving various actors, sometimes located in physically distant places, which form a value chain. The term 'value chain' (VC) describes the full range of activities that are required to bring a product or service from conception to the final consumer through the distinct phases of production, delivery, and final disposal after use (Kaplinsky & Morris, 2012). Different production stages are disaggregated along the value chain: a product can be thought and designed in one place, produced in another, and sold in a third. Accordingly, the value of a product is the sum of the various value-generating activities carried out by all the chain members, from the suppliers of raw materials to the sellers of the final good or service (Porter, 1980).

However, the value produced is not equally distributed along the chain, as illustrated by the concept of the 'smile curve'. In order to increase its revenues or consolidate its position, a firm may try to catch a higher share of this value, either from its suppliers or buyers, through innovations and bargaining activities (Brandenburger & Stuart, 1996). A firm can strengthen its bargaining power by introducing new selling channels or by training the sales staff (Almeida Costa & Zemsky, 2021); in addition, it can raise the value created by boosting its productivity, introducing new features to already developed products, selling complementary services, and lowering the cost structure through the innovation of its production process. More generally, changes in the firm's value creation, value delivery and value capture mechanisms can be

[1] We would like to express our sincere gratitude to Jasmine Mondolo for her assistance. Her attention to detail, suggestions, and dedication have significantly enhanced the quality of this work.

fostered by variations in the business model, either related to the production and internal organizational areas or the firm's external relations (Zott & Amit, 2010; Muller, Buliga & Voigt, 2018).

The business model concept is intrinsically linked to the exploitation of new opportunities (DaSilva & Trkman, 2014; George & Bock, 2011). Firms innovate their business to capitalize on these opportunities, such as those presented by new technologies (Chesbrough, 2010; Sabatier et al., 2012; Spieth et al., 2016; Zott et al., 2011). Business model innovation (BMI) can be triggered by the introduction of new elements, including disruptive technologies, that entirely reshape how a firm operates. In particular, the adoption of new technologies might have a powerful impact on firms' business models (Habtay & Holmén, 2014; Muller, Buliga & Voigt, 2018) and can prompt firms to innovate their way of doing business (Kiel et al., 2017; Muller, Buliga & Voigt, 2018; Bollwerg et al., 2020). Furthermore, the intensity of technology adoption leads to different degrees of business model changes (Ibarra et al., 2018).

As far as the concept of value capture is concerned, it has not received significant empirical support so far, mainly due to scant data availability and the difficulties in measuring this firm dimension. Consequently, evidence on the relationship between the latter and BMI is still limited. In this study, we try to fill this gap by assessing how changes in the business model, and in particular the introduction of new disruptive technologies, affect the firm's ability to appropriate the value produced along the value chain.

To this end, we resort to first-hand information on about 6,000 Italian small and medium-sized enterprises (SMEs) collected through an extensive survey administered at the end of 2019. The survey comprises 28 questions aimed at identifying the most relevant changes in the business model and the adoption of new technologies experienced in the previous years. Some questions also permit distinguishing between BMI related to internal activities and BMI attributable to external relations, while others disentangle technologies belonging to the managerial area, which we label 'management-related technologies', from technologies concerning the 'operational' area (i.e., the operations through which the factors of production are converted into output), which we label 'operation-related technologies'. Furthermore, firms were asked about the changes in the share of the value they captured along the vertical value chain. From the regression analysis, which is based on the estimation of a logit model, it emerges that both BMI and new technology adoption are positively associated with an increase in the firm's value share. This result particularly holds when changes in the business model activities concern the firm's external environment, and when technologies pertain to the operational area.

The balance of this work is organized as follows. Section 2 reviews the relevant literature; Section 3 illustrates the empirical strategy, the dataset, and the main variables; Section 4 discusses the results; Section 5 concludes.

2.   LITERATURE BACKGROUND

2.1   Value Chains and Value Appropriation

The way a firm interacts with the other players of the vertical value chain can affect its ability to capture the value produced. According to Gereffi et al. (2005), the choice of the relationship typology between buyer and supplier is determined by three factors, that is, the complexity of transactions, the codifiability of information, and the capability of suppliers. The interaction among these three factors leads to five typologies of value chain governance: in the *Market* typology, the buyer-supplier relationship is based on the market price; in the *Modular* typology, there is a tighter bond between firms than in the market typology due to the superior amount of information exchanged; in the *Relational* typology, the information shared between buyer and supplier is not easily transmitted or learned; lead firms specify what is needed and have some degree of control over suppliers. In the *Captive* typology, suppliers depend on one or few buyers, and the latter has a strong power asymmetry over the former. Finally, in the *Hierarchy* typology, there are strong vertical integration and managerial control by the lead firm on the supplier.

   In the meantime, several studies have explored the role played by governance typologies in firm performance. For instance, Brancati et al. (2017), who employ a sample of Italian firms observed between 2008 and 2013, find significant heterogeneity in innovation, productivity and sales growth among firms that occupy different positions along the value chain. In particular, a company involved in a relational bond with its buyers displays a higher probability of innovation, greater productivity, and sales growth than a firm engaged in other forms of value chain governance. In this respect, Liao & Marsillac (2015) report a positive link between supply chain flexibility and external knowledge acquisition; moreover, the value chain governance and its information distribution policy foster the capacity of a firm to transform external knowledge into innovation. In light of these considerations, in order to account for this potential source of heterogeneity and then properly study the effect of BMI and the introduction of new technologies on value appropriation, it may be advisable to control for governance typology as well.

2.2   Business Model Innovation

Among scholars, there is no clear definition of business model innovation (Lambert & Davidson, 2013; Foss & Saebi, 2017). Following Heikkilä and Bouwman (2018), we regard BMI as the activity or process in which core elements of the firm and its business logic are deliberately altered. The authors stress that many European SMEs engage in BMI; in particular, the authors study a sample of 1,597 companies and observe that, between 2016 and 2018, about 37 per cent of them have innovated their business model by changing their commercial partners or offering new products and services. In an even more dynamic environment, BMI is a critical source of competitive advantage (Casadesus-Masanell & Zhu, 2012; Amit & Zott, 2012), and one of the most important determinants of firm performance (Chesbrough & Rosenbloom, 2002). Several studies explore the effect of BMI on different firms' areas. Teece (2010) exploits the relationship between BMI and value creation, finding that the former can enhance the latter. Guo et al. (2017) posit that BMI mediates the positive relationship between opportunity recognition and firm performance. Also, Latifi and Bouwman (2018) show that BMI can influence firm performance directly or indirectly, and that this link is moderated by several factors, including firm and sectoral characteristics, productivity growth, revenue growth and changes in organizational capabilities.

Value capture is often regarded as one of the three components of the business model, along with value creation and value delivery (Muller, Buliga & Voigt, 2018). These three elements are not stand-alone factors, but are highly interconnected, so that an innovation in one element leads to some change in the other two (Zott & Amit, 2010; Muller, Buliga & Voigt, 2018). Hence, BMI can allow the company to enhance its value-capture ability and get larger shares of the value produced along the vertical value chain. However, the relationship between BMI and value capture ability has not been extensively explored, mainly because of the limited availability of data on value appropriation.

Accordingly, this work tries to fill this gap by answering the following research question:

RQ1. Does business model innovation play a role in fostering value appropriation along the vertical value chain?

Given the broad concept of BMI, to conduct a more fine-grained analysis, we decide to separately consider the changes in the business model concerning internal activities and the changes related to the external relationships. This distinction leads to the following question:

RQ1a. Are there any differences in the way the changes related to the internal areas of the firm and the changes concerning the external relationship affect the company's value capture ability?

2.3   New Technologies

In the last few decades, industrial systems have experienced an increasing spread of sophisticated digital technologies and applications, such as cyber-physical systems (CPS), Additive Manufacturing, augmented reality, robotics, remote monitoring, Artificial Intelligence, Big Data, Cloud Computing, and smart-connected products. These new technologies offer many business development opportunities. In this respect, Muller, Buliga and Voigt (2018) assert that Industry 4.0 would have a considerable impact on all the three main components of a business model (i.e., value creation, value delivery and value capture), which in turn help firms to fully reap the benefits deriving from the adoption of this new technologies. Industry 4.0 supports the introduction of new value-capture mechanisms through the monetization of innovations, which may foster firm performance. Gillani et al. (2020) show that the application of the principles of connectivity, automation, integration, computation, and the transformation of a firm into a smart one increases firm performance. Similar results are obtained by Muller, Fay & Brocke (2018), who report a positive effect of the implementation of Big Data Analytics on firm productivity. Moreover, Niebel et al. (2019) investigate the relationship between Big Data and innovation, and find that firms adopting Big Data are more prone to conduct product innovation, which in turn can foster sales. Additionally, Tang et al. (2018), who study the link between the Internet of Things (IoT) and firm performance, assert that the IoT has a positive impact mainly in the long term. This positive correlation between new technologies and performance also holds when the former take the form of Cloud Computing (Khayer et al., 2019), Business Intelligence (Chen & Lin, 2021) and management systems (Wieder et al., 2006). According to Parida et al. (2019), capturing value from the introduction of new technologies can lead to decreased costs, higher revenues, or the capture of new revenue streams. Furthermore, Rayna and Striukova (2016) show how additive manufacturing reshapes the firm's business model by reducing production and storage costs and changing the revenue structure through direct manufacturing. Finally, Kathuria et al. (2018) assess how Cloud Computing can enhance firm performance; the authors assert that value creation from Cloud Computing can be attributed to this technology's ability to reshape the value proposition from which customers can benefit, and which boosts firm performance and revenues.

To sum up, a relevant number of contributions have scrutinized the relationship between the introduction of new technologies and the cost and revenue dimension of the firm; however, limited attention has been given to the value capture dimension so far (Parida et al., 2019). In this study, we try to shed light on the relationship between the adoption of new technologies and the process of value capture by answering the following research question:

RQ2. Do new technologies play a role in fostering value appropriation along the value chain? In doing so, are operation-related technologies somehow different from management-related technologies?

3.   EMPIRICAL STRATEGY

3.1   The Empirical Model

To answer the research questions put forward in Section 2, we employ the following logit model:

$$y_i = \begin{cases} 1, & y_i > 0 \\ 0, & \text{otherwise} \end{cases} \tag{3.1}$$

$$y_i^* = \alpha BMI + \beta X_i + u_i \tag{3.2}$$

$$y_i^* = \alpha Tech\_Adoption + \beta X_i + u_i \tag{3.3}$$

where y_i represents the observed dependent variable (*d_ValueShare*), y_i^* is the associated latent variable, X_i is the vector of controls and u_i is the error term. In Eq. (2), the focal regressor is BMI (Business Model Innovation), while in Eq. (3), the key regressor is *Tech_Adoption* (capturing the technological adoption indexes). As the dependent variable is a dummy variable taking values zero and one, Eq. (2) and Eq. (3) are estimated using maximum likelihood logit regressions. The selected variables are described in Section 3.2.

3.2   Data and Variables

To perform the empirical analysis, we resort to first-hand information on about 6,000 Italian firms in the manufacturing and service sectors which we collected through an extensive survey. In addition to basic information on the innovation activities and technology adoption, we retrieve data on the type of relationship between the company and its major downstream partner (Humphrey & Schmitz, 2002; Gereffi et al., 2005), and also exploit questions on the share of value produced along the value chain acquired by the firm; specifically, companies were asked to report this share and indicate whether it had increased during the previous period. Then, we match survey data with financial data from the Bureau van Dijk – Aida database, which makes it possible to compute the performance measures. After some data cleaning, and after removing firms which did not fill the parts of the survey that are used in this analysis, we ended up with 4,902 observations.

Table 3.1 presents the main variables of the study, together with some descriptive statistics. The dependent variable (*d_ValueShare*) is a dummy that takes value 1 if the firm declared to have increased its share value, and 0 otherwise. We can note that 25.3 per cent of the sample companies reported an increase in their value share.

The key regressors can be divided into two main groups, namely, variables capturing BMI and variables concerning the adoption of new technologies. About the former, the survey contains 28 questions aimed at obtaining information about changes in business models. In particular, the number of changes reported measures the intensity of business model innovation captured by the variable *BMI_intensity*. Even though all the surveyed firms have supposedly made at least one change, none of them has reported changes in all the areas under scrutiny: the maximum number of changes is 25 over 28, while the average value of the variable *BMI_intensity* is 7.4. The questions related to BMI also focus on the two types of BMI previously illustrated, namely, the one related to changes in internal activities (e.g., product or process innovation), and the one concerning changes in external activities (e.g., buyer and seller relationships). We exploit this additional piece of information by adding the following focal regressors: *Internal_BMI*, which captures the sum of all the changes made in the product and process, finance and organizational areas, and *External_BMI*, which refers to the number of changes in the network/external relationships area. Figure 3.1 illustrates the firms' distribution by number of BM changes, and shows that most of the sampled companies have introduced a number of BMI changes ranging between 4 and 10. The last BMI-related variable included in the regressions is *Ext_over_int_BMI*, which consists of the ratio between *External_BMI* and *Internal_BMI* and helps assess which of the two types of BMI has the strongest association with the probability of augmenting the firm's value share. Specifically, a positive coefficient of this regressor would mean that external BMI is related to a higher likelihood of increasing the value share than internal BMI.

Regarding the technological variables, the survey allows us to develop four indexes (described in Table 3.1): *Tech_adoption* measures the number of technologies embraced by companies among the ten ones investigated in the survey (i.e., IoT and Big Data, Enterprise Resource Planning-ERP and similar systems, Business Intelligence and Customer Relationship Management-CRM, Cloud Computing, Cyber Security, interconnected and modular implants, Collaborative Robots, Additive Manufacturing, Wearable, Augmented Reality); it ranges from 0 to 10, which means there are both firms that have adopted all the ten technologies, and firms that have reported no technological adoption. The second technological variable, *Oper_tech*, considers only operation-related technologies, i.e., technologies that affect how firms run their business (i.e., IoT and Big Data, Cloud Computing, interconnected

Table 3.1   *Descriptive statistics*

Variable	Obs.	Mean	Median	Std. dev.	Maximum	Minimum
d_ValueShare	4,902	0.2537	0	0.4351	1	0
ShareValue	4,902	0.5034	0.5	0.3805	1	0
BMI_intensity	4,902	7.4203	7	4.2318	25	1
Internal_BMI	4,902	5.8491	5	3.2858	19	1
External_BMI	4,902	1.5711	1	1.3036	8	0
Ext_over_int_BMI	4,902	0.2787	0.25	0.2483	3	0
Employees2014	4,902	25.9220	9	240.1	12398	1
Age	4,902	16.7470	14	14.297	116	0
ROS_2014	4,902	4.9566	4.29	8.4057	29.94	-48.24
Expshare	4,902	0.1623	0.01	0.268	1	0
ShareDepCust	4,902	0.4487	0.4	0.2783	1	0
Tech_adoption	4,902	2.1013	2	1.8366	10	0
Oper_tech	4,902	0.6311	0	0.8611	5	0
Manag_tech	4,902	1.4700	1	1.2545	5	0
Oper_over_Manag	4,902	0.4250	0.33	0.5197	4	0
VC Relationship:						
Market	4,902	0.2031	0	0.4024	0	1
Modular	4,902	0.2475	0	0.4316	0	1
Relational	4,902	0.2600	0	0.4387	0	1
Captive	4,902	0.0587	0	0.2351	0	1
Hierarchy	4,902	0.2307	0	0.4213	0	1

Source: Authors' elaboration of data from our survey and Aida.

and modular implants, Collaborative Robots, and Additive Manufacturing), while *Manag_tech* refers to the adoption of management-related technologies (i.e., ERP and similar systems, Business Intelligence and CRM, Cyber Security, Wearable, Augmented Reality). The distribution of the sampled firms by number of adopted technologies is reported in Figure 3.2, from which it emerges that a significant amount of companies have not introduced any advanced technology yet, and that most of them have adopted a number of technologies that ranges between 1 and 3. Finally, the variable *Oper_over_ Manag* represents the ratio between *Oper_tech* and *Manag_tech*, which helps to understand the relative contribution of these two sets of digital technologies.

We also control for the firms' value share captured in 2019 along the value chain (*ShareValue*) and for some relevant firm characteristics. In particular,

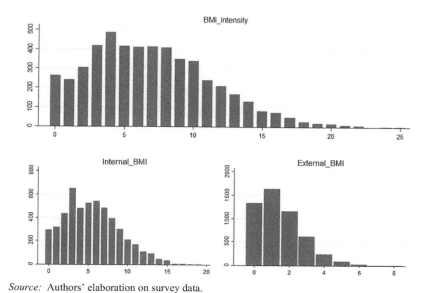

Source: Authors' elaboration on survey data.

Figure 3.1   Firms' distribution by number of BM changes

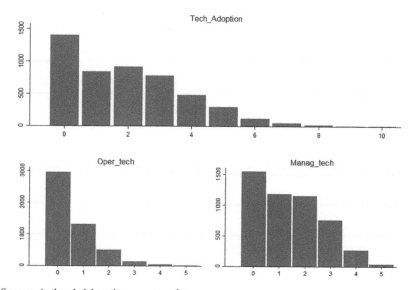

Source: Authors' elaboration on survey data.

Figure 3.2   Firms' distribution by number of adopted technologies

Employees2014 is the number of employees in 2014 and is a proxy of firm size, while the *Age* variable (measured in 2014) captures firm age, which is calculated as the difference between 2014 and the year of incorporation. The firm's financial performance is proxied by *ROS_2014*, which refers to the Return on Sales (ROS) in 2014; *Expshare* and *ShareDepCust* are the shares of revenues realized through exports and the part of revenues absorbed by the three major firm's customers, respectively. Finally, a set of variables (i.e., *Market, Modular, Relational, Captive* and *Hierarchy*) reflects the type of governance characterizing the relationship between the focal firm and its principal buyer (Gereffi et al., 2005). In this regard, as can be observed in Table 3.1, more than half of the sampled firms either engage in relational or modular links with downstream players. Also, about 20 per cent of companies conduct their business transactions at market prices, while 5.87 per cent and 23 per cent of them have their operations strictly or entirely controlled by the buyer, respectively.

4.   RESULTS OF THE REGRESSION ANALYSIS

This section presents the results of seven regressions based on the logit model introduced in Section 3. The estimates are reported in Table 3.2 and Table 3.3. In Table 3.2, Model 1 is the baseline model, where only the controls are included. Models 2–4 focus on business model innovation, while Models 5–7 investigate the impact of the adoption of new technologies. All the regression models contain sectoral dummies (defined at the NACE Rev2 3-digit level) and regional dummies to account for heterogeneity spurring from different regional policies and characteristics, as well as for sector-specific factors. Firms with a market relationship with their main buyers along the value chain are used as the default category.

The baseline model (Model 1 in Table 3.2) shows significant statistical evidence that having a *modular* or *relational* value chain relationship is associated with a higher probability of increasing the value share than the *market* one. Accordingly, a firm that engages in informational exchange with its buyers is more likely to increase the value appropriated along the value chain with respect to the other three types of relationships, namely, market, captive, and hierarchy. Market relationship, which is based on market price, is characterized by no informational exchange; thus, the firm is in horizontal competition with the other potential suppliers. Conversely, in captive and hierarchy business relationships, the supplier is strictly bound to the buyers, and its ability to make decisions is constrained by the player farther down the supply

Table 3.2   *Logit estimation (AME) – BMI*

Variables	Model 1	Model 2	Model 3	Model 4
	d_ValueShare	d_ValueShare	d_ValueShare	d_ValueShare
ShareValue	-0.0530***	-0.0578***	-0.0579***	-0.0528***
	(0.0168)	(0.0166)	(0.0166)	(0.0168)
BMI_intensity		0.0199***		
		(0.00139)		
External_BMI			0.0300***	
			(0.00585)	
Internal_BMI			0.0166***	
			(0.00233)	
Ext_over_int_BMI				0.0552**
				(0.0247)
Employees2014	-0.00175	-0.00979	-0.00952	-0.00132
	(0.00616)	(0.00606)	(0.00606)	(0.00616)
Age	-0.0442***	-0.0335***	-0.0337***	-0.0443***
	(0.00870)	(0.00863)	(0.00863)	(0.00870)
ROS_2014	5.86e-06	3.50e-05	4.02e-05	3.58e-05
	(0.000744)	(0.000733)	(0.000733)	(0.000745)
Expshare	0.0839***	0.0481**	0.0460**	0.0806***
	(0.0234)	(0.0232)	(0.0232)	(0.0234)
ShareDepCust	-0.0330	0.00264	0.00251	-0.0340
	(0.0240)	(0.0239)	(0.0239)	(0.0240)
VC relationship:				
Modular	0.0334*	0.0304*	0.0328*	0.0354*
	(0.0188)	(0.0183)	(0.0183)	(0.0188)
Relational	0.0329*	0.0269	0.0288	0.0337*
	(0.0190)	(0.0184)	(0.0184)	(0.0189)
Captive	-0.00721	-0.00677	-0.00612	-0.00735
	(0.0288)	(0.0281)	(0.0280)	(0.0287)
Hierarchy	-0.00463	0.0153	0.0173	-0.00279
	(0.0190)	(0.0190)	(0.0190)	(0.0190)
Industry sector	3 digits	3 digits	3 digits	3 digits
Regional Dummies	Yes	Yes	Yes	Yes
Obs.	4902	4902	4902	4902

Notes: Robust standard errors in parenthesis. ***, ** and * are p-value < 0.01, < 0.05 and < 0.1 respectively.

chain. Interestingly, the variables referring to firm size and firm performance are not significant. Conversely, being an exporter is associated with a higher probability of raising the value share, and this is consistent with other results found in the literature for Italian firms (e.g., Agostino et al., 2014). Model 1 of Table 3.2 also shows that older firms are less inclined to increment their value share. This can be ascribable to the well-known liability of the so-called senescence effect, according to which older firms are stuck in their routinized production processes and organizational structures, and are unwilling to adopt new strategies, while the youngest ones are more dynamic and prepared to reap the benefits of newness (Sørensen & Stuart, 2000; Coad, 2018). Moreover, the self-reported value of the share at the end of the period (*shareValue*) is negatively correlated with the likelihood of appropriating more value; this suggests that the firms that have declared a higher value share in 2019 are the same that exhibited zero growth in terms of value appropriated. Consequently, the companies that, at the beginning of the period, exhibit a lower share value are also the ones that experienced an increase in this variable, even though this growth was not sufficient to allow these firms to catch up with those showing higher values.

Model 2 studies the effect of changes in the business model by introducing the focal regressor *BMI_intensity* in the baseline regression. A high level of business model innovation intensity is positively associated with the probability of increasing the value share. Regardless of firm characteristics, the value chain typology, the physical location and the industrial sector of activity, business model changes may help the company appropriate a higher value along the value chain through changes in value creation, value offer and value appropriation mechanisms (Muller, Buliga & Voigt, 2018). In particular, the value creation mechanism can be modified by introducing new production processes, updating existing ones, and developing a new product or complementary services, while value appropriation can be enforced through bargaining strategies against the firm's sellers and buyers or by developing new sales systems and training of staff for negotiation function (Brandenburger & Stuart, 1996; Almeida Costa & Zemsky, 2021).

Model 3 analyses the disentangled effects of internal and external business model innovation, while Model 4 employs the variable *Ext_over_int_BMI* to exploit which kind of BMI is more related to the likelihood of increasing the value share along the value chain. Both internal and external BMI have a positive and statistically significant association with the increase in the value share. Thus, both changes in the value creation and value capture processes can result in two effective strategies for increasing the value appropriated. In Model 4, the coefficient of *Ext_over_int_BMI* is positive and statistically relevant, indicating that changes in the business model areas related to managing external relations are more likely to increase the value share than the internal organization and production processes. These results allow us to answer the first research question: in particular, changes in the business model have a positive association with the value share grasped from the value chain, and this particularly holds when changes pertain to how the company interacts with the external environment.

Table 3.3 shows the results of the logit regressions that focus on the role played by new technology adoption. Model 5 presents the baseline estimation augmented with the technology adoption index. The variable *Tech_adoption* displays a positive and statistically significant coefficient, implying that the more a firm invests in the adoption of new technologies, the higher the probability of observing a gain in the value share. This can be attributable to several factors, such as increasing productivity by reducing the number of inputs per output, which allows the firm to lower its costs and retain a larger share of value. New technologies can also reshape the revenue structure by creating new ways through which a company can appropriate a larger share of profit (Parida et al., 2019).

Like Model 3 in Table 3.2, Model 6 separately analyses the effects of the adoption of operation-related technologies and management-related technologies, while Model 7 assesses which type of technology is more relevant considering the value capture metrics. Estimates show that both these technology types are positively correlated with an increase in the firm's value share. For instance, management-related technologies, like business intelligence or enterprise resource planning systems, can help the firm to track its activity, save resources, or improve productivity, while operation-related technologies may also increase firm productivity by enhancing efficiency and reducing production costs and lead to establishing a competitive advantage over its rivals, which, in turn, can translate into higher prices, increased customer loyalty, and a greater capture of value along the value chain. Also, Model 7 shows that, compared to management-related technologies, introducing operation-related technologies allows the firm to capture a larger share of value.

To sum up, we detect a positive relationship between the new technology adoption and the value appropriated along the vertical chain, which especially holds with technologies pertaining to the operational area.

5.   CONCLUSIONS

While, in recent years, a sizable strain of literature has addressed the implications of BMI and the adoption of new technologies on firm performance, there is still a lack of evidence on the role played by these factors in a firm's ability to capture value from the value chain in which the firm is positioned.

Table 3.3   *Logit estimation (AME) – Technological adoption*

	Model 5	Model 6	Model 7
Variables	d_ValueShare	d_ValueShare	d_ValueShare
shareValue	-0.0597***	-0.0601***	-0.0840***
	(0.0162)	(0.0162)	(0.0204)
Tech_adoption	0.0272***		
	(0.00319)		
Oper_tech		0.0308***	
		(0.00788)	
Manag_tech		0.0251***	
		(0.00551)	
Oper_over_manag			0.0360**
			(0.0146)
Employees2014	-0.00722	-0.00726	-0.00776
	(0.00595)	(0.00595)	(0.00745)
Age	-0.0410***	-0.0406***	-0.0385***
	(0.00842)	(0.00843)	(0.0107)
ROS_2014	-0.000115	-0.000122	-0.000606
	(0.000711)	(0.000711)	(0.000929)
Expshare	0.0778***	0.0775***	0.0791***
	(0.0227)	(0.0227)	(0.0282)
ShareDepCust	-0.0161	-0.0166	-0.0422
	(0.0229)	(0.0229)	(0.0295)
VC relationship:			
Modular	0.0267	0.0267	0.0412*
	(0.0184)	(0.0184)	(0.0229)
Relational	0.0174	0.0179	0.0320
	(0.0184)	(0.0184)	(0.0227)
Captive	-0.0237	-0.0242	0.0221
	(0.0277)	(0.0277)	(0.0354)
Hierarchy	-0.00962	-0.00963	-0.00722
	(0.0185)	(0.0185)	(0.0238)
Industry sector	3 digits		
Regional Dummies	Yes		
Obs.	4902	4902	4902

Note: Robust standard errors in parenthesis. *** p-value < 0.01, ** p-value < 0.05, * p-value < 0.1.

This work aims to fill this gap, and empirically explores this relationship using first-hand, survey data on 4,902 Italian firms. We report evidence of a positive association between BMI and the ability to capture value from buyers and suppliers. Additionally, since the business model is a broad concept that embraces several business areas related to the production process, sales, and customer care, we group business model changes into two categories, namely internal and external. We find that internal and external changes are associated with an increase in the value captured by the firm, with BMI related to the external relations area showing the strongest correlation. Therefore, in a vertical context such as the value chain, adjusting the activities concerning the relationships with buyers and sellers can be regarded as an adequate strategy to improve the firm's value share along the chain.

Moreover, as disruptive technologies (e.g., Cloud Computing, Big Data Analytics, 3D Printing, and Collaborative Robots) provide firms with new opportunities to innovate their business model, we study how the introduction of these technologies relates to the ability of the firm to capture more value. We report a positive relationship between the introduction of new technologies and the increase in the firm's share value along the value chain. Finally, to get a more nuanced picture, we consider operation-related and management-related technologies separately; the regression analysis reveals that both of them have a positive relationship with the variable of interest, with operation-related technologies showing the strongest association.

This chapter thus advances our understanding of how a firm can retain a larger share of profits and increase its value capture ability. Specifically, it suggests that making adequate changes in the business model and adopting new technologies can represent the first step toward reaching this goal.

The main drawback of our study relies on the survey nature of the dataset, as the information used to build the variables of interest draws upon the companies' answers, which are self-evaluated and self-reported. Despite this limitation, we acknowledge that this contribution can spur further empirical investigation. Further research may also attempt to build a more robust measure of value capture and further delve into the BMI components in order to shed more light on the relationship between BM changes and the value captured by the company.

REFERENCES

Agostino, M., Giunta, A., Scalera, D., & Trivieri, F. (2014). The importance of being a capable supplier: Italian industrial firms in global value chains. *International Small Business Journal, 33*. doi:10.1177/0266242613518358.

Almeida Costa, A., & Zemsky, P. (2021). The choice of value-based strategies under rivalry: Whether to enhance value creation or bargaining capabilities. *Strategic Management Journal, 42*(11), 2020–2046. doi:https://doi.org/10.1002/smj.3282.

Amit, R., & Zott, C. (2012). Creating value through business model innovation. *MIT Sloan Management Review*, 41–49.

Bollwerg, L., Lackes, R., & Siepermann, M. W. (2020). Drivers and barriers of the digitalization of local owner operated retail outlets. *Journal of Small Business & Entrepreneurship, 32*(2), 173–201. doi:https://doi.org/10.1080/08276331.2019.1616256.

Brancati, E., Brancati, R., & Maresca, A. (2017). Global value chains, innovation and performance: Firm-level evidence from the Great Recession. *Journal of Economic Geography, 17*(5), 1039–1073. doi:https://doi.org/10.1093/jeg/lbx003.

Brandenburger, A. M., & Stuart, H. W. (1996). Value-based business strategy. *Journal of Economics & Management Strategy, 5*, 5–24. doi:https://doi.org/10.1111/j.1430-9134.1996.00005.x.

Casadesus-Masanell, R., & Zhu, F. (2012). Business model innovation and competitive imitation: The case of sponsor-based business models. *Strategic Management Journal, 34*, 464–482. doi:https://doi.org/10.1002/smj.2022.

Chen, Y., & Lin, Z. (2021). Business intelligence capabilities and firm performance: A study in China. *International Journal of Information Management, 57*, 102232. doi:10.1016/j.ijinfomgt.2020.102232.

Chesbrough, H. (2010). Business model innovation: Opportunities and barriers. *Long Range Planning, 43*, 354–363. doi:https://doi.org/10.1016/j.lrp.2009.07.010.

Chesbrough, H., & Rosenbloom, R. S. (2002). The role of the business model in capturing value from innovation: Evidence from Xerox Corporation's technology spin-off companies. *Industrial and Corporate Change, 11*(3), 529–555. doi:https://doi.org/10.1093/icc/11.3.529.

Coad, A. (2018). Firm age: A survey. *Journal of Evolutionary Economics, 28*(1), 13–43.

DaSilva, C. M., & Trkman, P. (2014). Business model: What it is and what it is not. *Long Range Planning, 47*(6), 379–389. doi:https://doi.org/10.1016/j.lrp.2013.08.004.

Foss, N. J., & Saebi, T. (2017). Business models and business model innovation: Between wicked and paradigmatic problems. *Long Range Planning, 51*, 9–21. doi:10.1016/j.lrp.2017.07.006.

George, G., & Bock, A. J. (2011). The business model in practice and its implications for entrepreneurship research. *Entrepreneurship Theory and Practice, 35*(1), 83–111. doi:https://doi.org/10.1111/j.1540-6520.2010.00424.x.

Gereffi, G., Humphrey, J., & Sturgeon, T. (2005). The governance of global value chains. *Review of International Political Economy, 78*, 78–104.

Gillani, F., Chatha, K. A., Jajja, M. S., & Farooq, S. (2020). Implementation of digital manufacturing technologies: Antecedents and consequences. *International Journal of Production Economics, 229*, 107748. doi:https://doi.org/10.1016/j.ijpe.2020.107748.

Guo, H., Tang, J., Su, Z., & Katz, J. A. (2017). Opportunity recognition and SME performance: The mediating effect of business model innovation. *R&D Management, 47*, 431–442. doi:https://doi.org/10.1111/radm.12219.

Habtay, S. R., & Holmén, M. (2014). Incumbents responses to disruptive business model innovation: The moderating role of technology vs. market-driven innovation. *International Journal of Entrepreneurship and Innovation Management, 18*(4), 289–309. doi:10.1504/IJEIM.2014.064211.

Heikkilä, M., & Bouwman, H. (2018). Business Model Innovation in European SMEs: Descriptive analysis of quantitative survey and case survey data. *Conference Proceedings* of the 31st Bled eConference Digital Transformation: Meeting the Challenges (pp. 543–560). Bled: University of Maribor Press. doi:10.18690/978-961-286-170-4.38.

Humphrey, J., & Schmitz, H. (2002). How does insertion in global value chains affect upgrading in industrial clusters? *Regional Studies, 36*(9), 1017–1027. doi:10.1080/0034340022000022198.

Ibarra, D., Ganzarain, J., & Igartua, J. I. (2018). Business model innovation through Industry 4.0: A review. *Procedia Manufacturing, 22*, 4–10. doi:https://doi.org/10.1016/j.promfg.2018.03.002.

Kaplinsky, R., & Morris, M. (2012). A Handbook for Value Chain Research. 113.

Kathuria, A., Mann, A., Khuntia, J., Saldanha, T. J., & Kauffman, R. J. (2018). A strategic value appropriation path for cloud computing. *Journal of Management Information Systems, 35*(3), 740–775. doi:https://doi.org/10.1080/07421222.2018.1481635.

Khayer, A., Talukder, M., Bao, Y., & Hossain, M. N. (2019). Cloud computing adoption and its impact on SMEs' performance for cloud supported operations: A dual-stage analytical approach. *Technology in Society, 60*. doi:10.1016/j.techsoc.2019.101225.

Kiel, D., Kai, C. A., & Voigt, I. (2017). The influence of the Industrial Internet of Things on business models of established manufacturing companies – A business level perspective. *Technovation, 68*, 4–19. doi:https://doi.org/10.1016/j.technovation.2017.09.003.

Lambert, S. C., & Davidson, R. A. (2013). Applications of the business model in studies of enterprise success, innovation and classification: An analysis of empirical research from 1996 to 2010. *European Management Journal, 31*(6), 668–681. doi:https://doi.org/10.1016/j.emj.2012.07.007.

Latifi, M.-A., & Bouwman, H. (2018). Business Model Innovation and Firm Performance: The role of mediation and moderation factors. *Conference Proceedings of the 31st Bled eConference Digital Transformation: Meeting the Challenges: June 17–20*, (pp. 67–83). Bled. doi:https://doi.org/10.18690/978-961-286-170-4.5.

Liao, Y., & Marsillac, E. (2015). External knowledge acquisition and innovation: The role of supply chain network-oriented flexibility and organisational awareness. *International Journal of Production Research, 53*(18), 5437–5455. doi:https://doi.org/10.1080/00207543.2015.1008106.

Muller, J., Buliga, O., & Voigt, K. (2018). Fortune favors the prepared: How SMEs approach business model innovations in Industry 4.0. *Technological Forecasting and Social Change, 132*(C), 2–17. doi:10.1016/j.techfore.2017.12.019.

Muller, O., Fay, M., & Brocke, J. v. (2018). The effect of big data and analytics on firm performance: An econometric analysis considering industry characteristics. *Journal of Management Information Systems, 35*(2), 488–509. doi:10.1080/07421222.2018.1451955.

Niebel, T., Rasel, F., & Viete, S. (2019). BIG data – BIG gains? Understanding the link between big data analytics and innovation. *Economics of Innovation and New Technology, 28*(3), 296–316. doi:10.1080/10438599.2018.1493075.

Parida, V., Sjödin, D., & Reim, W. (2019). Reviewing literature on digitalization, business model innovation, and sustainable industry: Past achievements and future promises. *Sustainability, 11*(2). doi: https://doi.org/10.3390/su11020391.

Porter, M. E. (1980). *Competitive Strategy: Techniques for Analyzing Industries and Competitors*. New York: Free Press.

Rayna, T., & Striukova, L. (2016). From rapid prototyping to home fabrication: How 3D printing is changing business model innovation. *Technological Forecasting & Social Change, 102*, 214–224. doi:https://doi.org/10.1016/j.techfore.2015.07.023.

Sabatier, V., Craig-Kennard, A., & Mangematin, V. (2012). When technological discontinuities and disruptive business models challenge dominant industry logics: Insights from the drugs industry. *Technological Forecasting and Social Change, 79*(5), 949–962. doi:https://doi.org/10.1016/j.techfore.2011.12.007.

Sørensen, J. B., & Stuart, T. E. (2000). Aging, obsolescence and organizational innovation. *Administrative Science Quarterly, 45*(1), 81–112.

Spieth, P., Schneckenberg, D. & Matzler, K. (2016), Exploring the linkage between business model (&) innovation and the strategy of the firm. *R&D Management, 46*: 403–413. https://doi.org/10.1111/radm.12218.

Tang, C.-P., Huang, T. C.-K., & Wang, S.-T. (2018). The impact of Internet of Things implementation on firm performance. *Telematics Informatics, 35*, 2038–2053.

Teece, D. J. (2010). Business models, business strategy and innovation. *Long Range Planning, 43*, 172–194. doi:https://doi.org/10.1016/j.lrp.2009.07.003.

Wieder, B., Booth, P., Matolcsy, Z. P., & Ossimitz, M.-L. (2006). The impact of ERP systems on firm and business process performance. *Journal of Enterprise Information Management, 19*(1), 13–29. doi:10.1108/17410390610636850.

Zott, C., & Amit, R. (2010). Business model design: An activity system perspective. *Long Range Planning, 43*(2), 216–226. doi:https://doi.org/10.1016/j.lrp.2009.07.004.

Zott, C., Amit, R., & Massa, L. (2011). The business model: Recent developments and future research. *Journal of Management, 37*(4), 1019–1042. doi:https://doi.org/10.1177/0149206311406265.

4. The effect of Big Data adoption on companies' selection of the target market

Jasmine Mondolo, Marco Cucculelli and Silvia Leoni

1. INTRODUCTION

In recent years, the term 'Big Data' has pervasively entered the working and academic spheres as a natural consequence of the growing role of digital technologies in our lives and the resulting growing amount of data collected. This unprecedented process of digitalization is not limited to the IT field; in fact, it pervades all sectors. The earliest definitions of Big Data are associated with the so-called 3V model (Laney, 2001), which is based on three defining properties: 'Volume' (regarding the enormous quantity of data that can be gathered), 'Velocity' (referring to the speed at which data are generated, stored and processed), and 'Variety' (in terms of types of data and data sources). This definition of Big Data has been later extended to comprise seven underlying criteria (Beyer & Laney, 2012). The new criteria that were not included in the original 3V model are 'Veracity' (which concerns the uncertainty in the data), 'Variability' (referring to changes in the meaning of the data), 'Visualization' (concerning the representability of complex data in a readable way), and 'Value' (related to the information that data provides).

The increasing level of digitalization within firms has prompted them to use data as a source of value creation, and this has possibly affected the traditional value chain (Porter, 1998). In particular, as explained by Faroukhi et al. (2020), this change has led to a shift from the traditional value-chain model to data-centric approaches, which characterize, for instance, the so-called Data Value Chain and Big Data Value Chain. Also, Big Data adoption and the presence of competencies in Big Data analytics (BDA) are found to positively affect firm performance, as documented by a large and heterogeneous strand of literature (e.g., Gupta & George, 2016; Wamba et al., 2017; Müller et al., 2018; Yadegaridehkordi et al., 2018; Niebel et al., 2019; Caputo et al., 2019;

Ferraris et al., 2019; Hallikainen et al., 2020; Behl, 2020; Bag et al., 2020; Ghasemaghaei, 2021; Muhammad et al., 2022).

Furthermore, many organizations trying to exploit the strategic business potential embedded in Big Data have started to renovate their business models or develop new ones, giving rise to the phenomenon of the so-called Big-Data business models (see Wiener et al., 2020 for a review of this nascent but promising body of research; for more recent contributions, see for instance Du et al., 2020, Ciampi et al., 2021, Dai & Liang, 2022, Chen, 2022). As far as business models are concerned, according to Osterwalder's popular business model framework (also known as Business Model Canvas), any business model is made up of nine so-called 'Building Blocks': the first one is labelled 'Costumer Segment Building Block' and concerns the target market of a company.[1] In particular, the niche market is intended as a very specialized customer segment in which the value proposition, the distribution channels and the relationships with customers are tailored to specific needs, and there is a close relationship between buyers and suppliers (Osterwalder & Pigneur, 2010).

Regarding niche markets, in the last few decades, the growing global competition has prompted many small and medium-sized enterprises (SMEs) to specialize their production and position themselves in narrow and well-defined market segments (Cedrola et al., 2009). The choice of operating in a niche market has been analysed from both the consumer side (Schaefers, 2014; Franke & Hader, 2014) and, more often, the supply side. For instance, some researchers have studied the properties of a niche market (Ivanov, 2009), the possible advantages of positioning in a restricted market segment (Dalgic & Leeuw, 1994), and the successful strategies adopted by firms to strive in these markets (Parrish et al., 2014, 2006).

Companies need to properly understand the rapid changes in their customers' preferences and purchasing habits in order to gain competitive advantage, as well as to face the challenges and grasp the opportunities brought about by globalization and the Industry 4.0 paradigm. As Big Data represent a reliable and critical source of knowledge about markets and customers, the proper use of BDA may help a company to gain an advantage in the existing competitive market, or to accurately identify new, less saturated markets. Importantly, the identification of a niche market can become the key to success especially for small enterprises (Nemati & Khajeheian, 2018).

The BDA-niche market nexus has been the object of a number of heterogeneous contributions (e.g., Nemati & Khajeheian, 2018; Masih & Joshi, 2021;

---

[1]   The other eight building blocks of Osterwalder's Business Model Canvas are: Channels; Customer relationship; Value proposition; Revenue streams; Key resources; Key activities; Key partnerships; Cost structure (Osterwalder & Pigneur, 2010).

Cillo et al., 2021; Varghese, 2021). However, to the best of our knowledge, a firm-level quantitative analysis specifically aimed to explore the role of Big Data adoption on a firm's selection of the target market, and in particular on the firm's decision to serve a niche market, has not been performed yet. This is likely to be at least partly attributable to limited data availability, and to the lack of consensus on a rigorous definition of 'niche market'.

This work tries to fill this gap by assessing whether and how the adoption of Big Data affects the probability of doing business in a specific market segment. To this purpose, it resorts to first-hand information collected through a unique survey administered to a large sample of Italian companies and covering a wide range of firms' aspects and decisions (e.g., business model innovation, adoption of digital technologies, adoption of green technologies, etc.). Additionally, it explores how this relationship is shaped by the company's prevailing type of production and the firm's position in the value chain, respectively. We find evidence of a positive link between Big Data technologies and the choice of serving a niche market, which is robust to the use of alternative variables capturing different Big-Data-related technologies. Finally, we observe that this relationship is moderated by the firm's main production type and its position within the value chain.

The balance of this chapter is organized as follows. Section 2 briefly reviews the pertinent literature. Section 3 describes the data, the model and the variables, and provides some descriptive statistics. Section 4 presents and discusses the results of the regression analysis. Section 5 concludes.

2.   LITERATURE REVIEW

In recent years, a sizeable body of literature has investigated the effect of Big Data adoption and the presence of competencies in Big Data analytics (BDA) on firm performance (e.g., Gupta & George, 2016; Wamba et al., 2017; Müller et al., 2018; Yadegaridehkordi et al., 2018; Niebel et al., 2019; Caputo et al., 2019; Ferraris et al., 2019; Hallikainen et al., 2020; Behl, 2020; Bag et al., 2020; Ghasemaghaei, 2021; Muhammad et al., 2022). As an illustration, Niebel et al. (2019) and Muhammad et al. (2022) analyze the relationship between the use of Big Data analytics and firm innovative performance in a sample of firms located in Germany and Pakistan, respectively. Behl (2020), who collects information from a survey administered to firms from both India and China, assesses how Big Data analytics capabilities of tech startups help them gain competitive advantage and improve their firm performance. Yadegaridehkordi et al. (2018) aim to identify and rank the drivers of the adoption of Big Data, and then to predict the influence of Big Data adoption on the performance of Malaysian manufacturing companies using a hybrid approach of decision-making trial and evaluation laboratory (DEMATEL)-adaptive neuro-fuzzy inference systems (ANFIS). Bag et al. (2020) apply Partial Least Squares Structural Equation Modelling (PLS-SEM) to survey-based data in order to examine the role of BDA management capabilities in innovative green product development and sustainable supply chain outcomes in South Africa. All in all, the aforementioned studies show that Big Data adoption typically exerts a positive effect on various types and measures of firm performance; interestingly, relevant attention is devoted to emerging economies, which are increasingly investing in digitalization and benefitting from such investment.

Meanwhile, various studies have recognized that BDA can play a role in the choice of the firm's target market, which is regarded as one of the components of the business model (Osterwalder & Pigneur, 2010). Specifically, a few qualitative studies address this topic focusing on some narrow economic fields; for instance, Masih & Joshi (2021) posit that Big Data analytics can help firms assess customer behaviour in the niche market of organic food in India. Cillo et al. (2021) investigate the importance for niche tourism destinations of investing in Big Data to improve their online reputation management and increase their competitiveness using a case-study methodology. In a similar vein, Varghese (2021) aims to better understand how smart tourism destinations could potentially enhance luxury tourism that is more personalized to meet visitors' unique needs and preferences, and discuss the technological opportunities offered by Big Data and social media analytics.

Also, some quantitative analyses partly relate to the topic under scrutiny, even though they do not specifically examine the impact of Big Data on firms' decision to 'go niche'. As an illustration, Broekhuizen et al. (2021) explore the nexus between digital platforms and platform openness (where the latter also includes openness towards customers) and examine the factors that should guide a company to choose between a mass and a niche market. In this regard, they posit that, in emerging or nascent markets, when turbulence is high and customer needs are relatively unknown, platforms do well by targeting a relatively small and homogenous niche. Kwon et al. (2021) empirically explore innovation patterns of Big Data technology in large companies and startups using patent information; they show that, unlike large firms, which tend to concentrate on business-to-consumer businesses (such as entertaining and interacting skills), startups and smaller firms focus on niche markets (such as materials, components and social media).

To sum up, the role of Big Data adoption in the firm's market selection, and especially in the decision to serve a niche market, has been gaining increasing attention. However, the extant literature is quite heterogeneous, and the few aforementioned quantitative studies tackle this issue only partially. In light of these considerations, this work attempts to shed more light on this topic by performing an empirical analysis based on microdata. In doing so, it adds to the literature on the implications of Big Data for firm performance and strategic choices, including the selection of the target market. Moreover, as it also accounts for the effect of the firms' position in the value chain, it extends our knowledge of the interplay between these three variables, which, to the best of our knowledge, have never been jointly analysed so far.

3.   EMPIRICAL STRATEGY

3.1   Data

The main data source for our analysis consists in a unique survey administered at the end of 2019 to a large sample of Italian companies operating in different sectors. In particular, we use the answers to this questionnaire to gather information on the type of market (mass vs. niche market) that a firm serves, the development and use of Big Data and related technologies, and two related variables (i.e., the number of data sources used and the origin of the data – i.e., whether they are produced internally). We rely on this survey to also recover information on the main type of production and the position in the value chain in which a firm operates, as well as to obtain information on the CEO (i.e., his/her tenure and whether he/she is an external member or a family member) and the strengthening of business skills (i.e., whether the firm has recently hired new employees with business skills). Then, we merge the survey data with balance-sheet firm-level information (i.e., firm age, number of employees and sector) from the commercial database Aida by Bureau van Dijk. After performing some data cleaning and removing firms for which most of the information is not available, we end up with a dataset comprising 6,164 observations.

3.2   Model and Variables

To assess how the adoption of Big Data and related technologies affects the firm's choice of serving a niche market, we estimate the following linear probability model (LPM):

$$Niche_i = \beta_0 + \beta_1 BigData_i + \beta_2 Z_i + f_i + u_i \qquad (4.1)$$

where $Niche_i$ is a binary variable that indicates whether the firm is addressing a niche market, $BigData_i$ is one or more key regressors capturing Big Data and related technologies, Z_i is a vector of firm-level controls, f_i is a set of Nace Rev2 2-digit sectoral fixed effects, and u_i is the error term. To control for heteroskedasticity, we compute robust standard errors.

In the second part of our analysis, we also interact the key regressor *Big Data$_i$* with the main type of production (*ProdType$_i$*) and the firm's position in the value chain (*ValueChain$_i$*), respectively:

$$Niche_i = \beta_0 + \beta_1 BigData_i ProdType_i + \beta_2 Z_i + f_i + u_i \qquad (4.2)$$

$$Niche_i = \beta_0 + \beta_1 BigData_i ValueChain_i + \beta_2 Z_i + f_i + u_i \qquad (4.3)$$

Table 4.1 reports the list of the variables and the baseline summary statistics. Concerning the key regressors, we include a set of dummy variables indicating, respectively, whether a firm is developing or using Big Data (including IoT and Industry Analytics) and whether a firm is developing or using three broad categories of digital technologies that are related to Big Data, namely, Big Data Management systems, Business Intelligence and CRM, and Cloud Computing. We also build the variable *Big-Data-related technologies: total*, which captures the number of Big-data related technologies a firm is developing or using, and the dummy variable *Big-Data-related technologies (tot) dummy*, reflecting whether a company is developing or using at least one of the four aforementioned technologies. In some specifications, we also introduce two additional variables that are related to the implementation of Big Data technologies, namely, the number of data sources and a dummy that indicates whether the firm produces its data internally.

To assess how the type of production and the position in the value chain affect the firm's probability to serve a mass market, both directly and through their interaction with the Big Data dummy, we resort to the variables *Type of production*, which comprises four categories – Components and semi-finished products', 'Final goods', 'Services', 'Systems and/or Modules (for complex products)' – and *Value Chain Position*, which includes five categories (i.e., 'Strongly dependent on clients', 'Production for the market', 'Production based on order but autonomous', 'Design and manufacturing in cooperation with the client', 'Client handles downstream activities'). Finally, we add some firm-level controls, namely *Employees, Firm age, CEO tenure* and *Non-family CEO* (i.e., a dummy indicating whether the CEO is a member of the family owning the firm).

Table 4.1 reports the list of the selected variables and the related baseline summary statistics. From this table, it emerges that about 37 per cent of the sampled firms operate in a niche market. Also, the most widespread Big-Data-related technology (which is developed or used by 39.4 per cent of the sampled companies) is Management systems. If we apply the narrowest definition of Big Data, we see that the percentage of firms currently developing or using this advanced technology is about 19 per cent. All in all, 56 per cent of the companies are developing or using at least one out of the four selected

Table 4.1   *Baseline summary statistics*

Variable	Obs.	Mean	Std. Dev.	Min	Max
Dependent variable					
Niche market	6,385	0.37	0.48	0	1
Key regressors: Big Data					
Big Data (including IoT and Industry Analytics)	6,995	0.19	0.4	0	1
Big-Data-related technologies: Management systems	6,995	0.39	0.49	0	1
Big-Data-related technologies: Business Intelligence and CRM	6,995	0.27	0.44	0	1
Big-Data-related technologies: Cloud Computing	6,995	0.31	0.46	0	1
Big-Data-related technologies: total	6,995	1.16	1.31	0	4
Big-Data-related technologies (tot) dummy	6,995	0.56	0.50	0	1
Big-Data-related controls					
Number of data sources	5,977	3.07	1.89	0	6
Data produced internally (dummy)	5,971	0.94	0.24	0	1
Moderators					
Type of production	6,995	2.60	0.73	1	4
Value chain position	6,995	2.68	1.25	1	5
Firm-level controls					
Employees	6,753	30.69	297.79	0	15684
Firm age	6,982	20.71	14.37	2	120
CEO tenure	6,995	14.83	12.07	1	120
Net profits	6,820	349.98	7,122.29		521.266
Business skills	6,385	0.21	0.41	0	1
Non-family CEO	6,995	0.17	0.38	0	1

technologies. Furthermore, on average, our selected companies employ three different data sources (with the number of data sources ranging from 0 to 6), and the large majority of them (94.1 per cent) produce data internally. Finally, we notice that, on average, the companies under scrutiny are relatively small – the mean number of employees being between 30 and 31 – and relatively young – the mean firm age being 20.7. It is also interesting to observe that only 17 per cent of the firms rely on a CEO who does not belong to the family owning the firm, thus remarking a peculiar trait of Italian companies, namely the significant widespread of family businesses.

Further formation on the adoption of Big Data is provided in Table 4.2, which reveals that almost 44 per cent of the sampled companies have not adopted any Big-Data-related technology yet, and that only about 8 per cent of the firms use all four of them. This suggests that, despite the pervasive wave of digitalization and technological progress we have been experiencing in recent years, several Italian firms are still struggling to keep up with this rapid and disruptive change. This result may be partly attributable to the fact that most of the surveyed companies (as well as most of the universe of Italian firms) are small or medium-sized family businesses, and it is likely that the rate of adoption of digital technologies among large and/or multinational companies is higher.

Table 4.2   *Firm distribution according to the number of types of Big-Data-related technology developed or used*

Number of types of Big-Data-related technology	Freq.	%
0	3,073	43.93
1	1,589	22.72
2	1,048	14.98
3	721	10.31
4	564	8.06
Total	6,995	100

Table 4.3 contains additional information on the two moderators. From Panel A of Table 4.3, we see that more than half of the sampled companies mainly engage in services, and that less than 5 per cent of them are specialized in the production of systems or modules. As far as the position in the value chain is concerned (Panel B, Table 4.3), the most representative category is 'Design and manufacturing in cooperation with the client' (25.59 per cent), followed by the category 'Strongly dependent on clients, (24.25 per cent); on the other hand, only 5.9 per cent of the sampled firms declared that the client does not take part in the manufacturing of the product, but handles the downstream activities.

Table 4.3   *Distribution of firms across type of production (a) and position in the value chain (b)*

Type of production (Panel A)	Freq.	%	Position in the value chain (Panel B)	Freq.	%
Components, semi-finished products	762	10.89	Strongly dependent on clients	1,696	24.25
Final goods	1,579	22.57	Production for the market	1,470	21.02
Services	4,378	62.59	Production based on order but autonomous	1,629	23.29
Systems and/or modules	276	3.95	Design and manufacturing in cooperation with the client	1,790	25.59
			Client handles downstream activities	410	5.86
Total	6,995	100			
			Total	6,995	100

4. RESULTS OF THE REGRESSION ANALYSIS

We start our analysis by running some LPM regressions in which we assess the role played by Big Data in the firms' decision to operate in a niche market. Table 4.4 reports the results of the estimation of equation (1). From all the six specifications, it emerges that the introduction of Big Data and related technologies positively affects the probability a firm has to serve a niche market. Specifically, in Model 1 we only use the key regressor based on a narrow definition of Big Data: we can say that, *ceteris paribus*, using or developing Big Data increases, on average, the probability to 'go niche' market by 11 percentage points (p.p.). Then, in Column 2 we add the dummies referring to the other three Big-Data-related technologies, which positively affect the probability of a firm to go niche too. Instead, in Column 3 we employ the indicator of technology intensity *Big-Data-related technologies: total*, which is positive and significant, suggesting that the higher the level of digitalization, the higher the probability of the company to choose a niche market rather than a mass market. This variable also represents the key regressor of Model 4, where two Big-Data-related controls are added, that is, the number of data sources and a dummy indicating whether the data are produced internally. While the first Big-Data-related control (as well as the indicator of technology intensity) positively impacts the probability of a firm to go niche, the second one is not significant; however, this result may be affected by the very low variability of this regressor within the sample, as the large majority (about 94 per cent) of the selected firms declared to produce data internally. All in all, our main finding, namely, the positive role played by Big Data and related technologies, is consistent with Nemati & Khajeheian's (2018) assertion that the application of Big Data helps companies obtain competitive advantage and identify the proper niche market.

Model 5 also includes the categorical variable *Type of production*. We can see that both the indicator of technology intensity (*Big-Data-related technologies: total*) and the variable *Number of Data Sources* are still highly significant and with positive sign. Regarding the prevalent production type, we see that, *ceteris paribus*, compared to firms who mainly produce components and semi-finished products (taken as the base category), the probability of a firm to 'go niche' is lower when the firm mainly engages in services.

Finally, Model 6 assesses the role of Big-Data-related technologies by controlling for the number of data sources and the firm's position in the value chain. As in Model 5, the key regressor and the variable *Number of Data Sources* are still highly and positively significant. Moreover, we can argue that, *ceteris paribus*, the probability of a firm serving a specific market segment is higher when the production is based on order but autonomous, and when design and manufacturing are made in cooperation, rather than when the firm is strongly dependent on the client (which is taken as the reference category).

Next, to provide a more nuanced and exhaustive picture of the Big-Data-niche market nexus, we test whether the probability of serving a niche market for the companies that have introduced Big Data technologies varies across different production types and different positions in the value chain. To this end, we interact the dummy capturing the adoption of Big-Data-related technologies with both the categorical variables *Type of production* and *Value Chain Position*. The results of this second set of regressions are presented in Table 4.5.

Model 1 of Table 4.5 contains the interaction between the dummy *Big-Data-related technologies (tot)* and *Type of production*. We can say that, for firms that produce components and semi-finished products (i.e., the production type taken as reference category), adopting Big Data-related technologies increases the firm's probability to 'go niche' by about 10 p.p. Additionally, among the Big-Data non-adopters Big-Data-related technologies – that is, firms for which the dummy *Big-Data-related technologies (tot)* equals zero – the companies that mostly engage in services (systems and/or modules) have a lower (higher) probability to serve a niche market than the producers of components and semi-finished products. Focusing on the interaction term, we can comment that, among those adopting Big-Data-related technologies, the companies that primarily supply systems and/or modules have a lower probability of going niche compared to those that mostly produce components and semi-finished products (i.e., the production type taken as the base category).

In Model 2 of Table 4.5, we interact the same Big Data dummy used in Model 1 with the categorical variable *Value Chain Position* and also control for the type of production. We see that, for those that are strongly dependent on the client (i.e., the value chain position taken as the reference category), adopting Big-Data-related technologies increases the firm's probability of going niche by about 15.8 p.p. However, the analysis of the interaction term suggests that there are significant differences across firms that occupy different positions in the value. Accordingly, in Model 3 we check whether a partly different picture emerges if we interact the variable *Value Chain Position* with a dummy that considers only the narrowest category of Big Data, rather than the previously used dummy (which relies on a broader definition of Big-Data-related technologies). Looking at the interaction term, we can see that firms that are strongly dependent on the client (taken as the reference category) have a higher probability of serving a niche market compared to companies that play a different role in the value chain (especially firms producing for the market and firms realizing design and manufacturing in cooperation with the client). This suggests that these companies, which already shape their products based on their clients' requests, are motivated to exploit the opportunities offered by BDA to further specialize and customize their production.

Finally, if we look at the firm-level controls in Table 4.4 and Table 4.5, we can posit that the company's probability of serving a niche market is higher the lower the number of employees and firm age, the higher the CEO tenure (even though this control is not always statistically significant), when the CEO is a family member and when the firm has strengthened its business skills. These results suggest that small, family firms that are managed by a CEO with some degree of experience and that have invested in business skills may find it profitable to address a specific market segment rather than a mass market.

5. CONCLUSIONS

With the advent of the Industry 4.0 paradigm, a significant number of companies have attempted to reap the benefits of the adoption of new digital technologies, including Big Data. The rapidly growing spread of this technology and the lively debate on the advantages and drawbacks brought about by the latest wave of technological progress have spurred a broad strand of literature on the drivers and implications of the adoption of Big Data and BDA. In particular, a relevant amount of studies have reported a positive effect of BDA on firm performance. Some contributions have instead scrutinized the impact of Big Data adoption on the corporate business model, whose reconfiguration can in turn boost firm performance. One of the main components, or 'building blocks' of business models consists in the firm's target market; notably, in the last few decades, the growing global competition has prompted several SMEs to specialize their production and position themselves in narrow and well-defined market segments, that is, in niche markets. As these companies

Table 4.4   *Results of the baseline Linear Probability Model regressions*

	(1)	(2)	(3)	(4)	(5)	(6)
	niche market	niche market	niche market	niche market	niche market	niche market
Big Data						
Big Data (dummy)	0.113***	0.062***				
	[0.017]	[0.019]				
Big Data-related technologies: Management systems (dummy)		0.032** [0.014]				
Big Data-related technologies: Business Intelligence and CRM (dummy)		0.031* [0.017]				
Big Data-related technologies: Cloud Computing (dummy)		0.080*** [0.015]				
Big Data-related technologies: total			0.050*** [0.005]	0.044*** [0.006]	0.044*** [0.006]	0.044*** [0.006]
Big Data-related controls						
Number of data sources				0.013*** [0.004]	0.011*** [0.004]	0.013*** [0.004]
Data produced internally (dummy)				-0.020 [0.027]		
Type of production (base cat.: components and semi-finished products)						
Final goods					-0.002 [0.024]	
Services					-0.069*** [0.026]	
Table 4.4 (Continued)						
Systems and/or Modules					0.060 [0.039]	
Value Chain Position (base cat: strongly dependent on the client)						

	(1)	(2)	(3)	(4)	(5)	(6)
Production for the market						-0.006
						[0.019]
Production based on order						0.034*
but autonomous						[0.019]
Design and						0.037**
manufacturing in						[0.018]
cooperation with the						
client						
Client handles marketing						0.034
and service						[0.030]
Firm-level controls						
Employees	-0.000***	-0.000***	-0.000***	-0.000***	-0.000***	-0.000***
	[0.000]	[0.000]	[0.000]	[0.000]	[0.000]	[0.000]
Firm age	-0.002***	-0.002***	-0.003***	-0.003***	-0.003***	-0.003***
	[0.000]	[0.000]	[0.000]	[0.000]	[0.000]	[0.000]
CEO tenure	0.001	0.001	0.001*	0.001*	0.001*	0.001*
	[0.001]	[0.001]	[0.001]	[0.001]	[0.001]	[0.001]
Business skills	0.094***	0.075***	0.073***	0.060***	0.061***	0.060***
	[0.016]	[0.016]	[0.016]	[0.017]	[0.017]	[0.017]
Non-family CEO	-0.057***	-0.058***	-0.058***	-0.056***	-0.053***	-0.057***
	[0.017]	[0.017]	[0.017]	[0.017]	[0.017]	[0.017]
Constant	0.550***	0.531***	0.531***	0.533***	0.539***	0.506***
	[0.081]	[0.080]	[0.081]	[0.090]	[0.090]	[0.088]
Industry FE	yes	yes	yes	yes	yes	yes
Observations	6,164	6,164	6,164	5,763	5,769	5,769

Note: Robust standard errors in brackets; *** $p < 0.01$, ** $p < 0.05$, * $p < 0.1$.

need to properly understand the rapid changes in their customers' preferences and purchasing habits, and Big Data represent a reliable and critical source of knowledge about markets and customers, a proper use of BDA may help a firm to accurately identify new, less saturated markets. Even though the extant literature seems to suggest that Big Data technologies can provide effective support to firms operating in niche markets, empirical evidence on the link between these two variables is still scant. In this chapter, we aim to fill this gap and, using firm-level first information retrieved from a unique survey, we investigate how the development and implementation of Big Data and related technologies affect a company's probability of 'going niche'.

Table 4.5   *Results of the Linear Probability Model regressions with interaction terms*

	(1)	(2)	(3)
	niche market	niche market	niche market
Big Data			
Big Data-related technologies (tot) dummy	0.100***	0.158***	
	[0.037]	[0.024]	
Big Data dummy			0.193***
			[0.038]
Type of production			
Final goods		0.001	-0.004
		[0.024]	[0.024]
Services		-0.073***	[0.026]
		[0.025]	
Systems and/or Modules		0.065*	0.067*
		[0.038]	[0.037]
Type of production			
Final goods	-0.007		
	[0.035]		
Services	-0.100***		
	[0.034]		
Systems and/or Modules	0.189***		
	[0.021]		
*Big Data-related technologies (tot) dummy * Type of production*			
Big Data * Final goods	0.017		
	[0.046]		
Big Data * Services	0.048		
	[0.040]		
Big Data * Systems and/or Modules	-0.155*		
	[0.083]		
Value Chain Position			
Production for the market		0.011	0.012
		[0.025]	[0.020]
Production based on order but autonomous		0.055**	0.035*
		[0.026]	[0.020]
Design and manufacturing in cooperation with the client		0.045*	0.053***
		[0.025]	[0.019]
Client handles marketing and service		0.071*	0.045
		[0.043]	[0.032]

	(1)	(2)	(3)
Big Data-related tech. (dummy) * *Value Chain Position*			
Big Data * Production for the market		-0.044	
		[0.035]	
Table 4.5 (Continued)			
Big Data * Production based on order but autonomous		-0.044	
		[0.035]	
Big Data * Design and manufacturing in cooperation with the client		-0.029	
		[0.034]	
Big Data * Client handles marketing and service		-0.067	
		[0.057]	
Big Data (dummy) * *Value Chain Position*			
Big Data * Production for the market			-0.137***
			[0.051]
Big Data * Production based on order but autonomous			-0.060
			[0.051]
Big Data * Design and manufacturing in cooperation with the client			-0.117**
			[0.048]
Big Data * Client handles downstream activities			-0.111
			[0.070]
Firm-level controls			
Employees	-0.000***	-0.000***	-0.000***
	[0.000]	[0.000]	[0.000]
Firm age	-0.003***	-0.003***	-0.002***
	[0.000]	[0.000]	[0.000]
CEO tenure	0.001*	0.001*	0.001
	[0.001]	[0.001]	[0.001]
Business skills	0.080***	0.079***	0.091***
	[0.016]	[0.016]	[0.016]
Non-family CEO	-0.054***	-0.055***	-0.054***
	[0.017]	[0.017]	[0.017]
Constant	0.540***	0.507***	0.562***
	[0.086]	[0.086]	[0.086]
Industry FE	yes	yes	yes
Observations	6,164	6,164	6,164

Note: Robust standard errors in brackets; *** $p < 0.01$, ** $p < 0.05$, * $p < 0.1$.

The regression analysis strongly suggests that the adoption of Big Data is positively related to a higher probability of serving a niche market, thus confirming the preliminary evidence provided by the extant literature. To account for the potential role of firm heterogeneity, we also examine how the relationship under scrutiny varies across different production types, as well as across different positions in the value chain. The regression estimates reveal that Big Data adopters that primarily supply systems and/or modules have a lower probability of going niche compared to those that mostly produce components and semi-finished products. Additionally, Big Data adopters that are strongly dependent on the client have a higher probability of serving a niche market compared to companies that play a different role in the value chain.

This study can provide useful directions to both companies and policymakers. In particular, based on these findings, companies that already serve a niche market, or intend to aim to a smaller and specific market segment, should be motivated to invest in the adoption of BDA, in the hiring of new employees with advanced technological skills and/or in the training of their current workers. Also, policymakers should support these firms, for instance, by providing them with funding, fiscal incentives and training courses. Finally, they can benefit from our evidence on the moderating role of the production type and the value chain, which can help them better identify the potential targets of their policies. Future research may conduct a similar analysis on a larger sample, examine the moderating effect of other variables or employ a broader array of digital technologies.

REFERENCES

Bag, S., Wood, L. C, Xu, L., Dhamija, P. & Kayikci, Y. (2020). Big data analytics as an operational excellence approach to enhance sustainable supply chain performance. *Resources, Conservation & Recycling*, 153, 104559.

Behl, A. (2020). Antecedents to firm performance and competitiveness using the lens of big data analytics: A cross-cultural study. *Management Decision*, 60(2), 368–398.

Beyer, M. A. & Laney, D. (2012) *The Importance of 'Big Data': A Definition*. Stamford, CT: Gartner.

Broekhuizen, T., Emrich, O., Gijsenberg, M., Broekhuis, M., Donkers, B. & Sloot, L. M. (2021). Digital platform openness: Drivers, dimensions and outcomes. *Journal of Business Research*, 122, Pages 902–914, ISSN 0148-2963, https://doi.org/10.1016/j.jbusres.2019.07.001.

Caputo, F., Cillo, V., Candelo, E. & Liu, Y. (2019). Innovating through digital revolution. The role of soft skills and Big Data in increasing firm performance. *Management Decision*, 57(8), 2032–2051.

Cedrola, E., Battaglia, L. & Tzannis, A. (2009). The Italian SMEs in the international context. A model to succeed in the global arena. Working Papers 52-2009, University of Macerata (Italy), Department of Finance and Economic Sciences.

Chen, W. (2022). Innovation of E-commerce Business Model Based on Big Data. In: Jansen, B. J., Liang, H. & Ye, J. (eds.) International Conference on Cognitive based

Information Processing and Applications (CIPA 2021). Lecture Notes on Data Engineering and Communications Technologies, vol. 84, Springer, Singapore, DOI: 10.1007/978-981-16-5857-0_43.

Ciampi, F., Demi, S., Magrini, A., Marzi, G. & Papa, A. (2021). Exploring the impact of big data analytics capabilities on business model innovation: The mediating role of entrepreneurial orientation. *Journal of Business Research*, 123, 1–13.

Cillo, V., Rialti, R., Del Giudice, M. & Usai, A. (2021). Niche tourism destinations' online reputation management and competitiveness in big data era: Evidence from three Italian cases. *Current Issues in Tourism*, 24(2), 177–191.

Dai, B. & Liang, W. (2022). The impact of Big Data technical skills on novel business model innovation based on the role of resource integration and environmental uncertainty. *Sustainability (Switzerland)*, 14(5), 2670.

Dalgic, T. & Leeuw, M. (1994). Niche marketing revisited: Concept, applications and some European cases. *European Journal of Marketing*, 28(4), 39–55.

Du, X., Gao, Y., Chang, L., Lang, X., Xue, X. & Bi, D. (2020). Assessing the application of big data technology in platform business model: A hierarchical framework. *PLoS ONE*, 15(9), e0238152.

Faroukhi, A. Z., El Alaoui, I., Gahi, Y. & Amine, A. (2020). Big Data monetization throughout Big Data value chain: A comprehensive review. *Journal of Big Data*, 7(1), 1–22.

Ferraris, A., Mazzoleni, A., Devalle, A. & Couturier, J. (2019). Big data analytics capabilities and knowledge management: Impact on firm performance. *Management Decision*, 57(8), 1923–1936.

Franke, N. & Hader, C. (2014). Mass or only 'niche customization'? Why we should interpret configuration toolkits as learning instruments. *Journal of Product Innovation Management*, 31(6), 1214–1234, DOI: 10.1111/jpim.12137.

Ghasemaghaei, M. (2021). Understanding the impact of big data on firm performance: The necessity of conceptually differentiating among big data characteristics. *International Journal of Information Management*, 57, 102055.

Gupta, M. & George, J. F. (2016). Toward the development of a big data analytics capability. *Information & Management*, 53, 1049–1064.

Hallikainen, H., Savimäki, E. & Laukkanen, T. (2020). Fostering B2B sales with customer big data analytics. *Industrial Marketing Management*, 86, 90–98.

Ivanov, M. (2009). Niche market or mass market? *Economics Letters*, 105(3), 217–220.

Kwon, O., Lim, S. & Lee, D. H. (2021). Innovation patterns of big data technology in large companies and start-ups: An empirical analysis. *Technology Analysis & Strategic Management*, 33(9), 1052–1067.

Laney, D. (2001). 3D Data Management Controlling Data Volume, Velocity and Variety. META Group Research Note, 6.

Masih, J. & Joshi, A. (2021). Understanding health-foods consumer perception using Big Data analytics. *Journal of Management Information and Decision Sciences*, 24(S3), 1–15.

Muhammad, A., Chen, Y., Aneela, Q., Waqar, A., Zahid, Y. & Fan, G. (2022). Big data analytics capability as a major antecedent of firm innovation performance. *The International Journal of Entrepreneurship and Innovation*, 23(4), 268–279.

Müller, O., Fay, M. & vom Brocke, J. (2018). The effect of Big Data and analytics on firm performance: An econometric analysis considering industry characteristics. *Journal of Management Information Systems*, 35(2), 488–509.

Nemati, S., & Khajeheian, D. (2018). Big Data for Competitiveness of SMEs: Use of Consumer Analytic to Identify Niche Markets. In: Khajeheian, D., Friedrichsen,

M., & Mödinger, W. (eds) *Competitiveness in Emerging Markets. Contributions to Management Science.* Springer, Cham, DOI: 10.1007/978-3-319-71722-7_29.

Niebel, T., Rasel, F. & Viete, S. (2019). BIG data – BIG gains? Understanding the link between big data analytics and innovation. *Economics of Innovation and New Technology,* 28(3), 296–316.

Osterwalder, A. & Pigneur, Y. (2010). *Business Model Generation: A Handbook for Visionaries, Game Changers, and Challengers.* Hoboken, NJ: John Wiley & Sons.

Parrish, E. D., Cassill, N. L., & Oxenham, W. (2006). Niche market strategy for a mature marketplace. *Marketing Intelligence & Planning,* 24(7), 694–707, DOI: 10.1108/02634500610711860.

Parrish, E. D., Cassill, N. L., Oxenham, W. & Jones, M. R. (2014). Modeling of niche market behavior of us textile and apparel firms. *Journal of Textile and Apparel, Technology and Management,* 4(2), 1–14, Available at: https://www.academia.edu/70707308/Modeling_of_Niche_Market_Behavior_of_US_Textile_and_Apparel_Firms (last access: 23.01.2024).

Porter, Michael E. (1998). Clusters and the new economics of competition. *Harvard Business Review,* 76(6), 77–90.

Schaefers, T. (2014), Standing out from the crowd: Niche product choice as a form of conspicuous consumption, *European Journal of Marketing,* 48(9/10), pp. 1805–1827. https://doi.org/10.1108/EJM-03-2013-0121.

Varghese, B. (2021). Digitization and Smart Tourism: Technological Opportunities For Luxury Tourism and Destination Image. In: *Handbook of Research on Future Opportunities for Technology Management Education,* DOI: 10.4018/978-1-7998-8327-2.

Wamba, S. F, Gunasekaran, A., Akter, S., Ji-fan Ren, S., Dubey, R. & Childe, S. J. (2017). Big data analytics and firm performance: Effects of dynamic capabilities. *Journal of Business Research,* 70, 356–365.

Wiener, M., Saunders, C. & Marabelli, M. (2020). Big-data business models: A critical literature review and multiperspective research framework. *Journal of Information Technology,* 35(1), 66–91.

Yadegaridehkordi, E., Hourmand, M., Nilashic, M., Shuiba, L., Ahanic, A. & Ibrahim, O. (2018). Influence of big data adoption on manufacturing companies' performance: An integrated DEMATEL-ANFIS approach. *Technological Forecasting & Social Change,* 137, 199–210.

5. Does business model innovation support high-growth firms?

Daniela Lena, Blendi Gerdoçi and Marco Cucculelli

1. INTRODUCTION

Scholarly interest in high-growth firms (HGFs) has increased primarily because of their potential impact on employment growth and economic development (Acs and Mueller, 2007; Acs et al., 2008; Henrekson and Johansson, 2010; Goswami et al., 2019; Flachenecker et al., 2020; Coad and Karlsson, 2022). Even though they represent a tiny minority of all firms, they are considered responsible for a disproportionate share of job creation (Henrekson and Johansson, 2010; Delmar et al., 2013; Coad et al., 2014), increased productivity (Du and Temouri, 2015), and innovation success (Hölzl and Friesenbichler, 2010). Moreover, these companies appear to have a high potential to generate long-term economic returns for shareholders and stakeholders (Coad et al., 2014; Senderovitz et al., 2016; Demir et al., 2017).

These positive attributes have led scholars to focus on understanding the factors and conditions that support this rapid growth (Coad et al., 2014). In the existing framework, elements such as human capital capabilities, corporate strategy, human resource management (HRM) practices, corporate innovativeness, and external elements beyond firms' control (e.g., industry fluctuations and macroeconomic changes) are identified as key drivers of HGF (Hölzl, 2009; Baum and Bird, 2010; Lopez-Garcia and Puente, 2012; Lee, 2014; Coad et al., 2014; Senderovitz et al., 2016; Borggren et al., 2016; Korsakienė et al., 2019; Anton, 2019). Nevertheless, there is still a knowledge gap in identifying the main drivers of firm growth (Gaikwad, 2022). Existing research appears to be heterogeneous from both the theoretical and methodological perspectives, leading to a patchy understanding of the circumstances and factors that set firms on a growth path.

Regarding business model innovation (BMI), while there is some evidence of the impact of BMI on firm performance, there is a paucity of research addressing the various mechanisms of BMI that drive value proposition, value creation, and value capture (Ramdani et al., 2019). In addition, identifying different approaches to value creation that go beyond product and process changes in BMI is still the focus of research (Shakeel et al., 2020).

Our study fits into the strand of literature on the relationship between BMI and HGF that addresses one or more dimensions of BMI (see, for instance: Goedhuys and Sleuwaegen, 2010; Rindova et al., 2012; Lee, 2014; Arregle et al., 2015; Najafi-Tavani et al., 2018; Peng et al., 2022; Caloghirou et al., 2022). In this context, our work aims to analyse the role of business model innovation in creating high business growth. Regarding BMI, we consider four dimensions, namely product and process innovation, the financial structure of business transactions, the transformation of business network relations of the firm, and the renewal of its organizational processes; these components enable BMI to define new ways of doing business and thus contribute to changes in existing industry competitiveness (Ireland et al., 2001).

Using a specific measure of growth performance, namely sales growth, and robust quantile regression approach (QR) (see Buchinsky, 1998), we show that some dimensions of BMI, such as network relationships and product and process innovation, contribute significantly to sales growth performance for high-growth firms. Conversely, organizational innovation seems to be very relevant only for slow- and moderate-growth firms, and the ability to generate revenue in novel ways (finance) shows a not-statistically significant relationship with HGFs.

The remainder of this chapter is organized as follows: Section 2 discusses the theoretical background and research hypotheses; Section 3 describes the data and the model used; Section 4 discusses the results of the regression analysis; Section 5 concludes.

2.   THEORETICAL BACKGROUND AND HYPOTHESES DEVELOPMENT

2.1   Conceptualization of High-growth Firms

High-growth firms (HGFs) are becoming increasingly important, and research on this topic has been significantly growing (Coad and Srhoj, 2020). Despite that, knowledge about the HGF concepts and definitions is patchy, and is mainly due to the heterogeneity of methodological approaches used to describe high growth and its measurement (Monteiro, 2019). Existing conceptualizations of HGFs can be broadly categorized based on the characteristics of the firms studied, the growth measure used, and the nature of growth (e.g., Wennberg, 2013; Coad et al., 2014; Demir et al., 2017; Gaikwad, 2022). The growth measure as a criterion for HGF is more common in research, but there is still disagreement among researchers. Specifically, to identify HGFs, some studies employ the relative annual growth, that is, the growth rate of the focal firm relative to the total population of firms in an industry, region, or country (Demir et al., 2017); other studies, instead, use absolute growth measures, where the firm's growth rate is measured as the difference between the beginning and the end of the observation period or as an annualized change over a period of time (Bos and Stam, 2014; Hendrickson et al., 2016). In both cases, the growth rate is calculated either in terms of employees, sales, or both. Another approach to defining HGF, which combines absolute and relative growth rates, has been proposed by scholars to remove the bias caused by firm size (small or large firms) (Gaikwad, 2022).[1]

2.2   The Drivers of High-growth Firms

Studies of what can be defined as a HGF have evolved steadily over time, and the literature is extensive but remains fragmented (Flachenecker et al., 2020). To give some examples, Demir et al. (2017) identify five drivers of high growth in their systematic review study, namely, human capital, corporate strategy, HRM practices, corporate innovation, and corporate capabilities for growth. These internal factors, over which the company has some influence, are considered to be good factors for the company's growth and competitiveness.

In a recent work, Gaikwad (2022), who reviews 60 articles on the topic, expands the number of drivers by including external factors beyond the control of the firm, such as industry and macroeconomic changes. According to the author, external elements such as industry affiliation and competitiveness, market demand, institutional framework, availability of finance, and technological development of the region contribute significantly to increasing the propensity to grow. However, it is still difficult to identify the conditions and factors that put companies on a growth path, as existing research is relatively heterogeneous.

Within the broad category of internal factors, many studies find that human capital emerges as the most important element in the strategic management of HGFs (Demir et al., 2017). In this context, the entrepreneur's capabilities, such as educational level and skills, professional experience (e.g., industry, market, and technology experience) and cognitive abilities, have a significant impact on growth prospects (Almus, 2002; Barringer et al., 2005; Hölzl, 2009;

---

[1]   The chosen measure has implications for research design, as studies focusing on relative growth tend to over-sample smaller firms, while studies focusing on absolute growth tend to over-sample larger firms (Delmar, 1997). One way to strike a balance between these approaches is to use a combination of relative and absolute growth rates or to use measures for defining minimum size criteria for inclusion in a study (Daunfeldt and Halvarsson, 2014; Daunfeldt et al., 2014).

Baum and Bird, 2010; Lopez-Garcia and Puente, 2012; Lee, 2014; Coad et al., 2014; Senderovitz et al., 2016; Korsakienė et al., 2019). Despite this consensus on the capabilities of entrepreneurs, results change depending on the study context (e.g., country, region, or industry affiliation); for example, some studies focusing on developed countries and high-tech industries report a significant and positive effect of the entrepreneur's education level on firm growth (e.g., Senderovitz et al., 2016; Savarese et al., 2016), while other studies from emerging economies find no effect (e.g., Hoxha and Capelleras, 2010; Goedhuys and Sleuwaegen, 2010). Concerning workers, several contributions have found a direct relationship between high levels of education and experience and firm's growth potential in developed countries (Lopez-Garcia and Puente, 2012; Arrighetti and Lasagni, 2013; Sirec and Mocnik, 2014). In contrast, for contexts such as Kosovo and the new members of the European Union, Hölzl (2009), Coad et al. (2014), and Borggren et al. (2016) document a negative relationship between high employee education and firm growth.

Within the array of internal growth factors, HRM practices, business innovation and internationalization are considered critical elements of a firm's strategy (Gaikwad, 2022). A significant impact of these three strategic choices on growth prospects has been identified in the literature (Barringer et al., 2005; Chan et al., 2006; Sims and O'Regan, 2006; Barbero et al., 2011; Coad et al., 2014; Lee, 2014; Ryzhkova, 2015; Borggren et al., 2016), but there is still a need for further research. Several researchers have noted a potential trade-off between high growth and HRM practices, that is, selection, training, and incentive compensation. For example, Fischer et al. (1997) and Coad et al. (2014) reported a potential trade-off between high growth and careful search and selection of personnel. Moreover, managerial compensation dispersion appears to have a negative impact on team decision-making ability, and thus on overall firm growth (e.g., Ensley et al., 2007; Parker et al., 2010). Also, Parker et al. (2010) emphasize the risk of innovation: according to the authors, HGFs that develop new products or services are less likely to survive, while those that have a single dominant product or service continue to grow. Similarly, Daunfeldt et al. (2016) highlight the complexity of the relationship between R&D and growth, which is most likely negative, and also find that industries with high R&D intensity tend to display a lower share of HGF.

In addition to internal factors, external environmental factors also appear to play an important role in increasing the propensity for HGF. Macroeconomic and industry-level factors also influence firm growth performance (Gaikwad, 2022); within industry-level factors, various studies investigate the effects of industry affiliation (Eckhardt and Shane, 2011), clustering (Arrighetti and Lasagni, 2013; Li et al., 2016; Giner et al., 2017; Kubičková et al., 2018), and competitiveness (Bos and Stam, 2014; Mazzucato and Parris, 2015) on the likelihood of rapid firm growth. Regarding the macroeconomic context, elements such as market demand (Arrighetti and Lasagni, 2013), positive economic conditions (Dragnić, 2014), and the interaction between formal and informal institutions (Lee, 2014; Krasniqi and Desai, 2016) are recognized as accelerators of high growth.

2.3   Research Hypotheses on the Link between BMI and Corporate High Growth

BMI refers to a company's ability to change its business model (BM) and the way it creates and captures value (Foss and Saebi, 2017). As a basis for BMI, companies change their structure to achieve optimal value proposition, creation, delivery, and capture (Geissdoerfer et al., 2016). These changes, triggered by technological shifts, changing customer preferences, or industry deregulation (Casadesus-Masanell and Zhu, 2013; Reddy and Reinartz, 2017), are achieved by transforming a single business model element (e.g., product/process, business network relationships, or organizational processes), changing multiple elements simultaneously, and/or changing the interactions between elements of a business model (Ramdani et al., 2019).[2]

The contribution of BMI to HGF has been studied in the existing literature considering only a single element of BMI (Rindova et al., 2012; Lee, 2014). In this context, the most commonly analysed dimension is the one related to the new products, services, and processes introduced to the market, that is, product and process innovations. The latter are generally assumed to be positively related to high growth (Lee, 2014), but the outcome seems to differ across economies, as does the role of product versus process innovation (Demir et al., 2017). For example, Goedhuys and Sleuwaegen (2010) show that product innovation is positively associated with high growth, but process innovation is not. In a later study in the Brazilian context, Goedhuys and Veugelers (2012) conclude that companies that only innovate processes without introducing new products risk becoming ineffective in increasing growth. Moreover, according to O'Regan et al. (2006) and Parker et al. (2010), product development may be less important for high growth. In this context, the potential links between firms' high growth and their product or process innovation remain poorly explored, and the existing results do not provide sufficient evidence for their role in HGF. Therefore, we put forward the following hypothesis:

H1: The 'product and process' dimension of business model innovation is positively associated with high-growth sales.

---

[2]   Moreover, changing one element will not only impact other elements but also the interactions between these elements (Kiron et al., 2013). Supporting this, Zott and Amit (2010), highlighted that innovative business models can be settled through connecting activities in a novel way that creates more value. Eyring et al. (2011) as well recommended that core business model elements need to be integrated in order to create and capture value.

The second dimension of BMI, known as finance, describes the ability to generate cash flow through innovative activities such as pricing policies aimed at mass or niche markets or increasing sales by introducing add-on or complementary services. Researchers have also highlighted the importance of financial capabilities for high growth (Gaikwad, 2022), but the existing studies focus on analysing how companies attract external financial capital rather than self-generated revenue growth. For example, Barbero et al. (2011) proxy financial capabilities with budgeting and cash flow management, availability of financial capital, financial reporting processes, financial statement analysis, and cost control; using these measures, they find a positive relationship between financial literacy and HGF. In addition, Moreno and Casillas' (2007) work reveals that this relationship is negatively correlated, but the higher the growth of the company, the more it relies on its ability to seize opportunities that require fewer financial resources. Therefore, we propose and test the following hypothesis:

H2: The 'finance' dimension of business model innovation is positively associated with high-growth sales.

The innovation of the commercial and business network represents another research area within the BMI dimension that is critical to the rapid development of the HGF. By integrating or outsourcing activities previously conducted upstream or downstream, modifying or introducing new direct distribution channels, and formalizing new partnerships with customers, suppliers, or competitors, this dimension of BMI supports new product development (Najafi-Tavani et al., 2018) and enables competitive advantage by achieving greater innovation (Freytag and Young, 2014). Business network relationships can provide valuable resources that entrepreneurs need to acquire and are critical for business growth (Arregle et al., 2015). Peng et al. (2022), in their study on the role of business networks, that is, organizational network and personal network, show that this dimension also acts as a good moderator for entrepreneurs' growth. Although there is consensus that the commercial and business network increases the propensity to grow, empirical evidence of this subject is still scant; in particular, the direct relationship between this BMI dimension and HGFs has not yet been studied. Therefore, we hypothesize the following:

H3: The 'commercial and business network' dimension of business model innovation is positively associated with high-growth sales.

The fourth dimension of BMI, that is, organizational innovation, is also expected to affect business growth. Effective organization of human resources or training and reorganization of business processes have great potential to increase business performance and growth (Gaikwad, 2022). In the literature, this dimension is analysed through the lens of personnel selection, training and incentive compensation. For example, some studies demonstrate that companies that focus on employees' training and development tend to have positive returns in terms of high growth (Barringer et al., 2005; Sims and O'Regan, 2006; Chan et al., 2006; Barbero et al., 2011). Borggren et al. (2016) posit that HGF should hire employees with complementary skills, as the employees' experience strongly influences the growth prospects of the organization. Recently, Caloghirou et al. (2022) show that employee training increases the likelihood that a firm will grow rapidly even in a struggling economy. Within this framework, we test the following hypothesis:

H4: The 'organization and processes' dimension of business model innovation is positively associated with high-growth sales.

3.   DATA AND METHODS

To study the emergence of HGFs, we use Italian data covering a large sample of Italian manufacturing firms. The data were collected between the second half of 2019 and the first two months of 2020 through a structured survey covering the whole country. Detailed information on the survey design and administration, as well as on the sample used for the analysis, can be found in the Appendix.

From an empirical point of view, given that the distributions of sales growth are fat-tailed and skewed (Coad and Rao, 2008), and following the recent literature (e.g., Coad and Rao, 2008; Coad et al., 2016; Herstad, 2018; Bianchini et al., 2018), we use the more robust QR approach (see Buchinsky, 1998) to assess the impact of different dimensions of BMI on sales growth. Importantly, such an approach allows us to identify potential asymmetric effects and variations in the coefficient estimates of HGFs (the upper quantiles) versus low-growth firms (the lower quantiles).

In our regression model, the dependent variable is the average annual log difference in sales over the 2016–2021 period. We exclude from the regression analysis the growth rate between 2020 and 2021 as it is very likely to be affected by the Covid-19 pandemic. The key regressors are the four indicators of BMI capturing the previously discussed dimensions, which are computed as the sum of several binary-coded indicators. We also include several control variables: following Coad (2009) and Coad et al. (2016), we account for input growth, which we proxy with employment and investment growth; we also add the lagged value (sales in 2016) to account for the convergence effect on sales growth. Due to limited data availability in our dataset, we use a dummy variable for R&D investment that identifies firms that did or did not invest in R&D in our base year (2016). Other control variables have been included in the regression model, such as the company age, the share of exports in total sales, and the 2-digit NACE sector. Finally, we calculated four indices for the respective BMI dimensions as the sum of the binary-coded indicators. A detailed description of all the variables and of the construction of the BMI indicators can be found in Table 5.1.

4.   RESULTS OF THE REGRESSION ANALYSIS

Table 5.2 presents the quantile results for the quantiles 0.05, 0.10, 0.25, 0.50, 0.75, 0.90 and 0.95. The regression results reveal that product and process innovation is positively associated with sales growth at the upper quantiles (95 per cent) and, surprisingly, also at the lower quantiles (5 and 10 per cent), although the results are not robust ($p < 0.1$). Moreover, the impact of this dimension of BMI on firm growth does not change significantly across quantiles. The second element of BMI, that is, finance innovation, does not have a significant impact on sales growth across quantiles. The third dimension of BMI, business relationship and business network innovation, is found to be positively related to sales growth at the top quantiles (90 and 95 per cent), whereas it is not significant in the lower quantiles. Moreover, the effect over the last two quantiles increases significantly. Finally, the innovation and organizational processes dimension of BMI is positively associated with sales growth only at the bottom and middle quantiles. For the upper quartile, that is, the high-growth companies, on the other hand, this dimension is not significant, even though it has a positive effect; the effect size for this dimension is stable across all quantiles.

All in all, the results suggest that some dimensions of business model innovation (e.g., business and business network relationships) make a significant contribution to corporate revenue growth only for high-growth companies, while others (e.g., organizational process innovation) are highly relevant for slow-growth companies.

Finally, our regression results provide interesting information on other determinants of growth. For instance, the dummy variable 'R&D' is not statistically significant. However, the estimated coefficients weaken at the upper quantiles. Consistent with recent empirical studies (Coad et al., 2016), the lagged absolute value of the dependent variable (LnSales) has no significant effect on firm sales growth at the lower quantiles (5 and 10 per cent), while it generally shows a negative and significant effect at the upper quantiles; moreover, the size of the negative impact is larger for the upper quantiles. Export

Table 5.1   *Description of the variables*

Variable	Description
$R\&Dt_{t-1}$	Dummy variable for spending in R&D activity
$LnSales_{t-1}$	The natural log of sales in 2016, the baseline year
$Exports_{t-1}$	Percentage of exports with respect to total sales
GrEmploy	Log of employment growth measured as the average of log-differences (period 2016–2020)
GrInvest	Log of capital growth measured as the average of log-differences (period 2016–2020)
Prod&Proc	A composite index that includes six indicators measuring the share of firms that have: (1) introduced new products; (2) enriched the main products with ancillary or complementary services; (3) specialized in a main product, extending its sale to markets or customers previously not served; (4) changed the customer base and the markets served; (5) introduced new and / or more efficient production processes; (6) decreased the 'Time to Market'.
Finance	A composite index that includes seven indicators measuring the share of firms that have (1) changed pricing policies (e.g., variable prices based on demand, discount systems, etc.); (2) changed the way products are sold (pay-per use, rental, lease, license or other systems); (3) increased the turnover thanks to the introduction of accessory or complementary services; (4) focused on mass markets; (5) focused on niche markets; (6) defined prices with a fixed price list; (7) defined prices dynamically (negotiation, price based on the available offer, auction).
BusNetw	A composite index that includes eight indicators measuring the share of firms that have (1) integrated activities previously carried out upstream (suppliers of raw materials, semi-finished products or machinery); (2) integrated activities previously carried out downstream (services, sales networks or customers); (3) integrated activities that support the main business; (4) outsourced activities previously carried out internally; (5) modified or introduced new direct sales channels (online, e-commerce or digital, new network of sale); (6) modified or introduced new indirect sales channels (wholesalers, distributors and other intermediaries); (7) formalized new partnerships with customers, suppliers or competitors; (8) benefited from incentives and / or tax breaks for investments in innovation.
Org&Proc	A composite index that includes seven indicators measuring the share of firms that have (1) added new job functions; (2) eliminated corporate job functions no longer needed; (3) added new skills and technological competences (hiring and / or training of personnel); (4) added new commercial skills and competences (hiring and / or training of personnel); (5) activated internal or external training courses for staff; (6) corporate processes reorganized; (7) changed the hierarchical levels.
LnAge	The natural log of number of years since foundation

activity is negatively related to sales growth, but only in lower quartiles. Our results also suggest that firm age is positively associated with growth, but only in lower quartiles, whereas it impacts negatively on growth in upper quartiles. Finally, employment and investment growth contribute positively to sales growth.

Table 5.2   *Quantile regression estimates for sales growth (100 bootstrap replications)*

	5%	10%	25%	50%	75%	90%	95%
	(1)	(2)	(3)	(4)	(5)	(6)	(7)
Prod&Proc	0.0476*	0.0331*	0.0028	0.0119	0.0029	0.0255	0.0489*
	(0.0282)	(0.0199)	(0.0105)	0.0077	(0.0106)	(0.0166)	(0.0277)
Finance	0.0562	0.0124	-0.0006	0.0063	0.0118	-0.0126	-0.0203
	(0.0377)	(0.0252)	(0.0134)	0.0100	(0.0107)	(0.0184)	(0.0269)
BusNetw	-0.0384	-0.0137	0.0120	0.0101	0.0145	0.0589**	0.0620*
	(0.0427)	(0.0276)	(0.0145)	0.0099	(0.0164)	(0.0232)	(0.0343)
Org&Proc	0.0311*	0.0433**	0.0361***	0.0317***	0.0327***	0.0214	0.0338
	(0.0087)	(0.0184)	(0.0093)	(0.0081)	(0.0095)	(0.0133)	(0.0260)
RDt_{t-1}	0.0092	.0039	0.0025	0.0002	-0.0020	0.0006	0.0030
	(0.0114)	(0.0068)	(0.0039)	(0.0029)	(0.0038)	(0.0060)	(0.0070)
$LnSales_{t-1}$	-0.0042	-0.0023	-0.0048**	-0.0072***	-0.0162***	-0.0240***	-0.0309***
	(0.0044)	(0.0038)	(0.0021)	(0.0015)	(0.0021)	(0.0029)	(0.0041)
$Exports_{t-1}$	-0.0013***	-0.0008***	-0.0003**	-0.0001*	0.0001	0.0001	0.0001
	(0.0003)	(0.0002)	(0.0001)	(0.0001)	(0.0001)	(0.0001)	(0.0002)
GrEmploy	0.4228***	0.3894***	0.4058***	0.4337	0.4542***	0.4516***	-0.0309***
	(0.0417)	(0.0377)	(0.0248)	(0.0181)	(0.0259)	(0.0287)	(0.0041)
GrInvest	0.1694***	0.1810***	0.1777***	0.1705***	0.1909***	0.1979***	0.2257***
	(0.0290)	(0.0198)	(0.0114)	(0.0101)	(0.0139)	(0.0193)	(0.0225)
LnAge	0.0311***	0.0095	-0.0029	-0.0076**	-0.0164***	-0.0228***	-0.0297***
	(0.0087)	(0.0074)	(0.0046)	(0.0032)	(0.0035)	(0.0044)	(0.0084)
Constant	-0.4110***	-0.2458***	-0.1071***	0.0192	0.1731***	0.2919***	0.3848***
	(0.0849)	(0.0493)	(0.0235)	(0.0174)	(0.0208)	(0.0266)	(0.0396)
Pseudo-R2		0.1727	0.1771	0.2102	0.2583	0.3163	0.3481
Observations				4,669			

Note: Standard errors in parentheses; *** $p < 0.01$, ** $p < 0.05$, * $p < 0.1$.

5.   CONCLUSIONS

There has been a significant increase in interest in studying what makes a company an HGF. Research has identified elements such as human capital capabilities, corporate strategy, HRM practices, corporate innovativeness, and external elements beyond corporate control as key determinants of HGFs. In this chapter, we investigate whether the four identified dimensions of BMI, which leads companies to pursue new ways of doing business that help improve industry competitiveness and performance, have a positive effect on HGFs.

Using sales growth as a specific measure of growth performance and the QR approach, we show that two of the dimensions of business model innovation, that is, business network relationships and product and process innovation, contribute significantly to firm sales growth performance. In contrast, organizational innovation appears to be very important only for slow-growth firms. Finally, the ability to generate revenue in novel ways (finance) has a non-significant effect on high firm growth.

Hence, this study should advance our knowledge of the relationship between BMI and high-growth companies. However, it presents some limitations that could be addressed by future research. One of these drawbacks is the relatively small sample size and the specific context; second, the growth indicator represented by turnover is measured as an average annual log difference for the period between 2016 and 2021; even if we exclude the growth rate from 2020 to 2021, it is still possible to find bias in the growth rates due to the Covid-19 pandemic. Finally, the structure and changes of the business model are recovered by a questionnaire based on a self-reported assessment of the most important changes, which only partially captures the intensity of innovation in each of the four main dimensions of the BMI.

REFERENCES

Acs, Z.J., Mueller, P. (2008). Employment effects of business dynamics: Mice, gazelles and elephants. *Small Business Economics*, 30(1), pp. 85–100. https:// doi .org/ 10 .1007/s11187-007-9052-3.

Acs, Z.J., Parsons, W., Tracy, S. (2008). High-impact firms: Gazelles revisited. In Washington, DC: An office of advocacy working paper. U.S.: Small Business Administration (SBA).

Almus, M. (2002). What characterizes a fast-growing firm? *Applied Economics*, 34(12), pp. 1497–1508, DOI: 10.1080/00036840110105010.

Anton, S.G. (2019). Leverage and firm growth: An empirical investigation of gazelles from emerging Europe. *International Entrepreneurship and Management Journal*, 15, pp. 209–232. https://doi.org/10.1007/s11365-018-0524-5.

Arregle, J., Batjargal, B., Hitt, M.A., Webb, J.W., Miller, T., Tsui, A.S. (2015). Family ties in entrepreneurs' social networks and new venture growth. *Entrepreneurship Theory and Practice*, 39(2), pp. 313–344. https://doi.org/10.1111/etap.12044.

Arrighetti, A., Lasagni, A. (2013). Assessing the determinants of high-growth manufacturing firms in Italy. *International Journal of the Economics of Business*, 20(2), pp. 245–267, DOI: 10.1080/13571516.2013.783456.

Barbero, J.L., Casillas, J.C., Feldman, H.D. (2011). Managerial capabilities and paths to growth as determinants of high-growth small and medium-sized enterprises. *International Small Business Journal*, 29, pp. 671–694.

Barringer, B.R., Jones, F.F., Neubaum, D.O. (2005). A quantitative content analysis of the characteristics of rapid-growth firms and their founders. *Journal of Business Venturing*, 20(5), pp. 663–687.

Baum, J.R., Bird, B.J. (2010). The successful intelligence of high-growth entrepreneurs: Links to new venture growth. *Organization Science*, 21, pp. 397–412.

Bianchini, S., Pellegrino, G., Tamagni, F. (2018). Innovation complementarities and firm growth. *Industrial and Corporate Change*, 27(4), pp. 657–676.

Borggren, J., Eriksson, R.H., Lindgren, U. (2016). Knowledge flows in high-impact firms: How does relatedness influence survival, acquisition and exit? *Journal of Economic Geography*, 16(3), pp. 637–665. https://doi.org/10.1093/jeg/lbv014.

Bos, J.W.B., Stam, E. (2014). Gazelles and industry growth: A study of young high-growth firms in The Netherlands, *Industrial and Corporate Change*, 23(1), pp. 145–169, https://doi.org/10.1093/icc/dtt050.

Buchinsky, M. (1998). Recent advances in quantile regression models: A practical guideline for empirical research. *Journal of Human Resources*, pp. 88–126.

Caloghirou, Y., Giotopoulos, I., Kontolaimou, A., Tsakanikas, A. (2022). Inside the black box of high-growth firms in a crisis-hit economy: Corporate strategy, employee human capital and R&D capabilities. *International Entrepreneurship and Management Journal*, 18, pp. 1319–1345. https://doi.org/10.1007/s11365-020-00674-x.

Casadesus-Masanell, R., Zhu, F. (2013). Business model innovation and competitive imitation: The case of sponsor-based business models. *Strategic Management Journal*, 34(4), pp. 464–482.

Chan, Y.E., Bhargava, N., Street, C.T. (2006.) Having arrived: The homogeneity of high-growth small firms. *Journal of Small Business Management*, 44, pp. 426–440.

Coad, A., Rao, R. (2008). Innovation and firm growth in high-tech sectors: A quantile regression approach. *Research Policy*, 37(4), pp. 633–648.

Coad, A. (2009) *The Growth of Firms: A Survey of Theories and Empirical Evidence*. Edward Elgar Publishing Ltd., Cheltenham.

Coad, A., Daunfeldt, S.-O., Hölzl, W., Johansson, D., Nightingale, P. (2014). High-growth firms: Introduction to the special section. *Industrial and Corporate Change*, 23, pp. 91–112.

Coad, A., Segarra, A., Teruel, M. (2016). Innovation and firm growth: Does firm age play a role? *Research Policy*, 45(2), pp. 387–400.

Coad, A., Srhoj, S. (2020). Catching gazelles with a lasso: Big data techniques for the prediction of high-growth firms. *Small Business Economics*, 55, pp. 541–565. https://doi.org/10.1007/s11187-019-00203-3.

Coad A., Karlsson, J. (2022). A field guide for gazelle hunters: Small, old firms are unlikely to become high-growth firms. *Journal of Business Venturing Insights*, 17.

Daunfeldt, S.-O., Halvarsson, D. (2014). Are high-growth firms one-hit wonders? Evidence from Sweden. *Small Business Economics*, 44, pp. 361–383.

Daunfeldt, S.-O., Elert, N., Johansson, D. (2014). The economic contribution of high-growth firms: Do policy implications depend on the choice of growth indicator? *Journal of Industry, Competition and Trade*, 14, pp. 337–365.

Daunfeldt, S.-O., Elert, N., Johansson, D. (2016). Are high-growth firms overrepresented in high-tech industries? *Industrial and Corporate Change*, 25, pp. 1–21.

Delmar, F. (1997). Measuring growth: Methodological considerations and empirical results. In: Donckels, R., Miettinen, A. (Eds.), *Entrepreneurship and SME Research: On Its Way to the Next Millennium*. Ashgate, Aldershot, England, pp. 199–216.

Delmar, F., McKelvie, A., Wennberg, K. (2013). Untangling the relationships among growth, profitability and survival in new firms. *Technovation*, 33, pp. 276–291.

Demir, R., Wennberg, K., McKelvie, A. (2017). The strategic management of high-growth firms: A review and theoretical conceptualization. *Long Range Planning*, 50, pp. 431–456.

Dragnić, D. (2014). Impact of internal and external factors on the performance of fast-growing small and medium businesses. *Management: Journal of Contemporary Management Issues*, 19(1), pp. 119–159.

Du, J., Temouri, Y. (2015). High-growth firms and productivity: Evidence from the United Kingdom. *Small Business Economics*, 44, pp. 123–143.

Eckhardt, J.T., Shane S.A. (2011). Industry changes in technology and complementary assets and the creation of high-growth firms. *Journal of Business Venturing*, 26(4), pp. 412–430.

Ensley, M.D., Pearson, A.W., Sardeshmukh, S.R. (2007). The negative consequences of pay dispersion in family and non-family top management teams: An exploratory analysis of new venture, high-growth firms. *Journal of Business Research*, 60, pp. 1039–1047.

Eyring, M.J., Johnson, M.W., Nair, H. (2011). New business models in emerging markets. *Harvard Business Review*, 89(1), pp. 89–95.

Fischer, E., Reuber, A.R., Hababou, M., Johnson, J.P., Lee, K. (1997). The role of socially constructed temporal perspectives in the emergence of rapid-growth firms. *Entrepreneurship Theory and Practice*, 22.

Flachenecker, F., Gavigan, J.P., Goenaga, X., Pasi, G., Preziosi, N., Stamenov, B., Testa, G. (2020). High growth enterprises: Demographics, financing and policy measures. JRC Technical Report. Joint Research Centre. Brussels, Belgium. https:// ec.europa.eu/jrc/en/publication/highgrowthenterprisesdemographicsfinancepolicy -measures (accessed 15 January 2024), pp. 13–30.

Foss, N.J., Saebi, T. (2017). Fifteen years of research on business model innovation: How far have we come, and where should we go? *Journal of Management*, 43(1), pp. 200–227.

Freytag, P., Young, L. (2014). Introduction to special issue on innovations and networks: Innovation of, within, through and by networks. *Industrial Marketing Management*, 43(3), pp. 361–364.

Gaikwad, P. (2022). Catching up with gazelles: A systematic literature review of high growth antecedents. In: Becker-Ritterspach, F., Dörrenbächer, C., Tomenendal, M. (Eds.), *The Promises and Properties of Rapidly Growing Companies: Gazelles*, Emerald Publishing Limited, Bingley, pp. 7–38. https://doi.org/10.1108/978-1 -80117-818-120221002.

Geissdoerfer, M., Bocken, N.M.P., Hultink, E.J. (2016). Design thinking to enhance the sustainable business modelling process – a workshop based on a value mapping process. *Journal of Cleaner Production*, 135, pp. 1218–1232.

Giner, J.M., Santa-María, M.J., Fuster, A. (2017). High-growth firms: Does location matter? *International Entrepreneurship and Management Journal*, 13, pp. 75–96. https://doi.org/10.1007/s11365-016-0392-9.

Goedhuys, M., Sleuwaegen, L. (2010). High-growth entrepreneurial firms in Africa: A quantile regression approach. *Small Business Economics*, 34, pp. 31–51.

Goedhuys, M., Veugelers, R. (2012). Innovation strategies, process and product innovations and growth: Firm-level evidence from Brazil. *Structural Change and Economic Dynamics*, 23, pp. 516–529.

Goswami, G., Medvedev, D., Olafsen, E. (2019). *High-Growth Firms*. World Bank Publications – Books, The World Bank Group, nr. 30800.

Hendrickson, L., Bucifal, S., Balaguer, A., Hansell, D. (2016). Employment dynamics of Australian entrepreneurship: A management perspective. *Technology Innovation Management Review*, 6(6), pp. 33–40. http://timreview.ca/article/995.

Henrekson, M., Johansson, D. (2010). Gazelles as job creators: A survey and interpretation of the evidence. *Small Business Economics*, 35(2), pp. 227–244.

Herstad, S.J. (2018). Product innovation and employment growth at the firm level: A quantile regression approach to inter-industry differences. *Applied Economic Letters*, 25(15), pp. 1062–1065.

Hölzl, W. (2009). Is the R&D behaviour of fast-growing SMEs different? Evidence from CIS III data for 16 countries. *Small Business Economics*, 33, pp. 59–75.

Hölzl, W., Friesenbichler, K. (2010). High-growth firms, innovation and the distance to the frontier. *Economics Bulletin, Access Econ*, 30(2), pp. 1016–1024.

Hoxha, D., Capelleras, J.L. (2010). Fast-growing firms in a transitional and extreme environment: Are they different? *Journal of Small Business and Enterprise Development*, 17(3), pp. 350–370. https://doi.org/10.1108/14626001011068671.

Ireland, R.D., Hitt, M.A., Camp, S.M., Sexton, D.L. (2001). Integrating entrepreneurship and strategic management actions to create firm wealth. *The Academy of Management Executive*. 15(1), pp. 49–63.

Kiron, D., Kruschwitz, N., Haanaes, K., Reeves, M., Goh, E. (2013). The innovation bottom line. *MIT Sloan Management Review*, 54(2), pp. 1–20.

Korsakienė, R., Kozak, V., Bekešienė, S., Smaliukienė, R. (2019). Modelling internationalization of high growth firms: Micro level approach. *Business Administration and Management*, XXII(1), pp. 54–71. doi:10.15240/tul/001/2019-1-004.

Krasniqi, B.A., Desai, S. (2016). Institutional drivers of high-growth firms: Country-level evidence from 26 transition economies. *Small Business Economics*, 47, pp. 1075–1094. https://doi.org/10.1007/s11187-016-9736-7.

Kubičková, V., Krošláková, M., Michálková, A., Benešová, D. (2018). Gazelles in services: What are the specifics of their existence in Slovakia? *Management & Marketing, Sciendo*, 13(2), pp. 929–945.

Lee, N. (2014). What holds back high-growth firms? Evidence from UK SMEs. *Small Business Economics*, 43, pp. 183–195.

Li, M., Goetz, S.J., Partridge, M., Fleming, D.A. (2016). Location determinants of high-growth firms. *Entrepreneurship & Regional Development*, 28(1–2), pp. 97–125, DOI: 10.1080/08985626.2015.1109003.

Lopez-Garcia, P., Puente, S. (2012). What makes a high-growth firm? A dynamic probit analysis using Spanish firm-level data. *Small Business Economics*, 39, pp. 1029–1041.

Mazzucato, M., Parris, S. (2015). High-growth firms in changing competitive environments: The US pharmaceutical industry (1963 to 2002). *Small Business Economics*, 44, pp. 145–170, https://doi.org/10.1007/s11187-014-9583-3.

Monteiro, G.F.A. (2019). High-growth firms and scale-ups: A review and research agenda. *RAUSP Management Journal*, 54(1), pp. 96–111.

Moreno, A.M., Casillas, J.C. (2007). High-growth SMEs versus non-high-growth SMEs: A discriminant analysis. *Entrepreneurship & Regional Development*, 19(1), pp. 69–88, DOI: 10.1080/08985620601002162.

Najafi-Tavania, S., Najafi-Tavani, Z., Naudéc, P., Oghazie, P., Zeynaloof, E. (2018). How collaborative innovation networks affect new product performance: Product innovation capability, process innovation capability, and absorptive capacity. *Industrial Marketing Management*, 73, pp. 193–205.

O'Regan, N., Ghobadian, A., Gallear, D. (2006). In search of the drivers of high growth in manufacturing SMEs. *Technovation*, 26, pp. 30–41.

Parker, S.C., Storey, D.J., Van Witteloostuijn, A. (2010). What happens to gazelles? The importance of dynamic management strategy. *Small Business Economics*, 35, pp. 203–226.

Peng, H., Li, B., Liu, Y. (2022). How social network influences the growth of entrepreneurial enterprises: Perspective on organizational and personal network. *SAGE Open*, pp. 1–16. DOI: /10.117 https://doi.org/10.1177/21582440221108170/215824402211081.

Ramdani, B., Binsaif, A., Boukrami, E. (2019). Business model innovation: A review and research agenda. *New England Journal of Entrepreneurship*, 22(2), pp. 89–108.

Reddy, S.K., Reinartz, W. (2017). Digital transformation and value creation: Sea change ahead. *GfK Marketing Intelligence Review*, 9(1), pp. 10–17. https://doi.org/10.1515/gfkmir-2017-0002.

Rindova, V.P., Yeow, A., Martins, L.L., Faraj, S. (2012). Partnering portfolios, value-creation logics, and growth trajectories: A comparison of Yahoo and Google (1995 to 2007). *Strategic Entrepreneurship Journal*, 6, pp. 133–151.

Ryzhkova, N. (2015). Does online collaboration with customers drive innovation performance? *Journal of Service Theory and Practice*, 25, pp. 327–347.

Savarese, M.F., Orsi, L., Belussi, F. (2016). New venture high growth in high-tech environments. *European Planning Studies*, 24(11), pp. 1937–1958, DOI: 10.1080/09654313.2016.1232700.

Senderovitz, M., Klyver, K., Steffens, P. (2016). Four years on: Are the gazelles still running? A longitudinal study of firm performance after a period of rapid growth. *International Small Business Journal*, 34, pp. 391–411.

Shakeel, J., Mardani, A., Chofreh, A.G., Goni, E.A., Klemeš, J.J. (2020). Anatomy of sustainable business model innovation. *Journal of Cleaner Production*, 261, 121201.

Sims, M.A., O'Regan, N. (2006). In search of gazelles using a research DNA model. *Technovation*, 26, pp. 943–954.

Sirec, K., Mocnik, D. (2014). Indicators of high potential firms' rapid growth: Empirical evidence for Slovenia. *Transformations in Business & Economics*, 13(2A)(32A), pp. 448–461.

Wennberg, K. (2013). Managing high-growth firms: A literature review. International Workshop on Management and Leadership Skills in High-Growth Firms. https://www.oecd.org/cfe/leed/Wennberg_Managing %20a %20HGF .pdf (accessed 15 January 2024).

Zott, C., Amit, R. (2010). Business model design: An activity system perspective. *Long Range Planning*, 43(2–3), pp. 216–226.

6. The role of business models in explaining differences in firm performance

Riccardo Cappelli and Marco Cucculelli

1. INTRODUCTION

The debate over the factors that influence firm success is always at the forefront of the strategic management literature. A considerable amount of literature examines the relative roles of industries' effects and firms' strategic resources and capabilities in explaining firm heterogenous performance (Rumelt, 1991; McGahan and Porter, 1997; Andersen, 2011). These analyses reflect the two dominating paradigms, namely, the strategic positioning paradigm (Porter, 1985) and the resource-based view (Wernerfelt, 1984; Barney, 1991).

A recent stream of literature emphasizes the relevance of the business model (BM) in determining firm performance (Afuah and Tucci, 2001; Zott and Amit, 2008; Nair et al., 2012). The development and diffusion of information and communication technologies (ICT), and especially the Internet, have amplified the need for businesses to change how they target consumers, and have also affected the ways to capture value from products and services (Zott et al., 2011). The emergence of the so-called e-business model has, for example, has challenged the traditional model based on the in-store business. New BMs can emerge also in low-tech industries; the Gillette's razor and blade model is a well-known example of how BMs might confer a competitive advantage over rivals.

Even though the literature on the effect of the BM on firm performance is growing, most of the empirical contributions rely on case studies (Amit and Zott, 2012) or focus on a single industry (Bigliardi et al., 2005). As a consequence, the results of these studies are hardly generalizable, and, more importantly, fail to disentangle the independent effect of BM from industry and firm-level effects. In addition, the existing literature mostly focuses on large firms and start-ups (Malone et al., 2006; Velu, 2015), thus neglecting the most prevalent corporate size class worldwide, that is, the small and medium-sized firms (SMEs). This chapter aims to fill these gaps by analysing the role of BM on firm performance in established SMEs, which, together with industry and firm-level effects, is regarded as one of the three key determinants of performance.

For this purpose, we need to face the empirical challenge of the identification of business models. Specifically, we propose a general applicable (cross-industries) methodology to identify and classify BMs starting from the financial statements of companies. Data from financial statements contain a wide range of information which reveals elements of the BMs adopted by firms. For example, information on the firm's intangible assets allows us to grasp the importance of knowledge capital and to discern whether the firm relies on formal innovation activities (i.e., R&D activities) to create value in the form of improved products (product innovations); the length of the credit cycle, instead, signals whether a firm sells their products directly to consumers or to wholesalers. In general, if two firms show differences in one element, or in a combination of more elements, it is reasonable to assume that these two firms have different BMs (Lanzolla and Markides, 2021).

Using balance sheet data for 1,156 SME Italian firms operating in nine manufacturing industries, we clustered firms into BMs. Through the cluster analysis, we identify from six to nine distinct BMs per industry, and a total of 65 BMs. Next, we exploit the hierarchical structure of the data, with firms nested within BMs and BMs nested within industries, to analyse how much of the variance of firm performance is accounted for by BMs. The results of the mixed-effects linear regressions show that BM effects range between 11 and 43 per cent depending on the measure of firm performance. In general, we find that, as expected, the firm effect is the strongest one, but also that the BM effect outweighs the industry effect.

The rest of this book chapter is organized as follows. Section 2 briefly reviews the pertinent literature; Section 3 describes the data and methods; Section 4 illustrates and discusses the results of the empirical analysis. Section 5 concludes.

2.   LITERATURE BACKGROUND

The concept of business model has been receiving increasing attention from academics. Following an initial period marked by the emergence of multiple business model definitions that only partially overlap (Zott et al., 2011), there has recently been a certain convergence in viewing business models as a set of interconnected activities directed by the firm itself and its stakeholders (e.g., customers, suppliers).

While the importance of BMs in determining firm success by the theoretical literature has received wide acknowledgement in the theoretical literature

(Afuah, 2004; Casadesus-Masanell and Ricart, 2011), empirical research on
the relationship between BM and firm performance is still scant (Wirtz et al.,
2016); most scholars have relied primarily on case studies to demonstrate how
specific configurations of BMs allow firms to outperform rivals (Magretta
2002; Morris et al., 2006). Other researchers have conducted quantitative analyses on large samples of firms, but their studies have been limited to certain
industries such as banking (DeYoung, 2005) and biotechnology (Glick, 2008;
Sabatier et al., 2010). For example, Morris et al. (2013), using a survey of
Russian food service firms, show that the type of selected BM helps to explain
higher performance. A few studies have used cross-industry data to examine
the relationship between BM and firm performance. As an illustration, Malone
et al. (2006), using data on publicly traded US corporations, identify 16 BMs,
and find that some of them outperform others. Also, Zott and Amit (2007),
who employ survey data on entrepreneurial firms with Internet-based BMs,
report that BM novelty is a driver of the market value of entrepreneurial firms.

   To summarize, from the literature it emerges that BMs help to explain the
heterogeneous performance of companies; however, the existing studies do not
take into account the combined effect of firm, BM, and industry-level features.
Our analysis attempts to fill this gap.

3.   EMPIRICAL STRATEGY

3.1   Sample

We use BvD-AIDA data on a Italian manufacturing SMEs[1] for the period
2008–2017. To perform our analysis, we consider industries that comprise
more than 100 firms. Specifically, the sample used for our analysis is made
up of 1,156 companies operating in nine NACE 4-digit industries (Table 6.1).

3.2   Identification of the Business Models

One of the main aims of this study consists in the identification of the BMs. To
this end, we first construct a set of variables which capture the driving factors
of a firm's ability to create and capture value and, more in general, of a firm's
way of operating (see Table 6.2). For example, a high share of intangible assets
(*Intangible*) signals that knowledge and innovations matter for firms' value
creation. Moreover, the intensity of R&D expenditure (*R&D*) tells us how
much of the ability to create value through the pursuit of innovation is driven

---

[1]   We regard as SMEs all the enterprises whose sales revenues in 2008 amounted
between 5 million and 50 million euro.

Table 6.1   *List of sectors included in the analysis*

NACE Code	Description
1051	Operation of dairies and cheese making
1520	Manufacture of footwear
2222	Manufacture of plastic packing goods
2229	Manufacture of other plastic products
2511	Manufacture of metal structures and parts of structures
2550	Forging, pressing, stamping and roll-forming of metal; powder metallurgy
2562	Machining
2599	Manufacture of other fabricated metal products nec
2829	Manufacture of other general-purpose machinery nec

Table 6.2   *List of variables used to identify the BMs*

R&D	R&D and Advertising expenditure / Total assets
Intangible	Intangible assets / Total assets
Vertical integration	Value added / Sales
Complexity	External services / Sales
Human capital	Salaries and wages / Number of employees
Labour intensity	Number of employees / Total physical assets
Pricing	Sales / Number of employees
EBITDA margin	EBITDA / Sales
Asset turnover ratio	Sales / Total assets
Physical assets	Physical assets / Total assets
Credit	Length (number of days) of the credit cycle
Debit	Length (number of days) of the debit cycle
Commercial	Length (number of days) of the commercial cycle

by formal R&D activities. The ratio between value-added and sales is used to proxy vertical integration (*Vertical Integration*) and, thus the firm's degree of control over the value chain. Also, the length of the credit cycle (*Credit*) may permit disentangling firms operating in different value chains; in particular, firms selling their products to persons (B2C) are, in general, characterized by shorter credit cycles than business-to-business (B2B) firms.

Next, to identify BMs, we conduct a cluster k-means analysis on the 13 variables previously selected (with the values observed for the year 2008). Cluster analysis is performed nine times, that is, one for each of the manufacturing industries under scrutiny. In doing so, we end up with 65 clusters, with the number of clusters per industry ranging from six to nine.

3.3   Firm Performance

When we assess the contribution of BMs to firm performance, we separately proxy the latter with several variables which are expected to capture different aspects of firm performance, namely: sales per capita (i.e., the ratio between sales and the number of employees; *Sales pc*), value-added per capita (i.e., the ratio between value-added and number of employees; *Value Added pc*), the return on assets (*ROA*), the return on sales (*ROS*), and the return on investments (*ROI*). For instance, we can reasonably assume that *Sales pc* refers more to value creation than to value capture, while *ROS* mainly concerns value capture rather than value creation.

3.4   The Econometric Model

In order to analyse the influence of business models on performance, we use hierarchical models (Bryk and Raudenbush, 1992), which allow us to determine how much variation in a variable is accounted for by each level of the hierarchy. Specifically, we employ this model to assess the impact of firms (level 1) nested within BMs (level 2) nested within industries (level 3). We estimate the following equation for each variable measuring firm performance:[2]

$$Performance_{ijk} = \mu + \alpha_j + \beta_{jk} + \varepsilon_{ijk} \tag{6.1}$$

where $Performance_{ijk}$ is one of the five measures of performance of firm i in BM j and industry k. This model allows us to estimate how much of the variance of $Performance_{ijk}$ is explained at each level of analysis (i.e., firm, BM and industry level).

4.   RESULTS OF THE EMPIRICAL ANALYSIS

4.1   Descriptive Evidence

In the first part of this section, we present some descriptive statistics on the influence of BMs on firm performance. Figure 6.1 shows the share of industry value-added (in percentage terms) in 2008 and 2017 by BM for two of our nine industries. Comparing the values of the two years, we see that the BM clusters display different dynamics. As for the industry '1051 – Operation of dairies and cheese making' (see panel a), the industry value-added share

---

[2]   To estimate equation [1], we use the MIXED command provided in STATA software (Mehmetoglu and Jakobsen, 2017).

increases by 31.1 per cent for BM '1' (from 20.0 per cent in 2008 to 26.3 per cent in 2017) and decreases by 21.8 per cent for BM '2' (from 18.6 per cent in 2008 to 14.4 per cent in 2017). We also observe significant changes in the ranking; for instance, in the case of sector '2550 – Forging, pressing, stamping and roll-forming of metal; powder metallurgy' (see panel b), the BM with the highest industry value added share in 2008 is the BM '41', while the BM with the highest share in 2017 is the BM '44'.

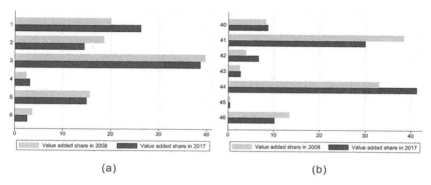

(a)   (b)

Figure 6.1   *Industry value added share by BM: panel (a) Industry NACE code: 1051; panel (b) Industry NACE code: 2550*

Figure 6.2 shows the growth rates between 2008 and 2017 in the BMs' share of industry value added and the BMs' share of industry sales for two industries (i.e., '1051 – Operation of dairies and cheese making' and '2229 – Manufacture of other plastic products'). It is interesting to note that these two indicators are often significantly different in terms of magnitude, and that there are also cases of divergence in the time dynamics (see, e.g., BM '4' in panel (a), and BM '25' in panel b).

In general, from the descriptive statistics, different dynamics across BMs emerge (in particular, growing BMs versus declining BMs); additionally, these dynamics vary with the indicator used. This hints at the presence of a complex relationship between BM and firm performance which is worth investigating.

4.2   Value Creation and Value Capture by BMs

As a further step to analyse whether BMs show different dynamics, we consider two crucial aspects of BMs, that is, value creation and value capture. Accordingly, following Verdin and Tackx (2015), we map our BMs into four quadrants based on their performance in terms of value creation and value capture. In line with the existing literature, we use firms' sales per capita

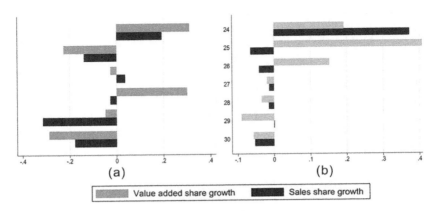

Figure 6.2   *Growth rates between 2008 and 2017 (%) in the value added*
              and sale industry shares by BM: panel (a) Industry NACE
              code: 1051; panel (b) Industry NACE code: 2229

growth rates to proxy value creation, and firms' ROS growth rate as a measure
of value capture. Finally, we use the median value of the observed firm growth
rates from 2008 to 2017 to determine a BM's location on the map.

Panel (a) of Figure 6.3 maps the 65 BMs into the four categories. We see
that the BMs are distributed across all the quadrants, thus confirming the heterogeneous performance of BMs within and between economic performance
indicators. Panel (b) shows the same distribution of panel (a), but only for the
industry '2829 – Manufacture of other general-purpose machinery nec'; as
before, BMs span over all the quadrants.

4.3   Variance Component Analysis

To examine the impact of BMs on company performance, we use multilevel
mixed-effects linear regressions. Table 6.3 shows the percentage of variability
associated with each of the three levels, namely businesses, BMs, and industries. For each measure of firm performance, the first three columns refer to
the analysis performed using annual values (period 2009–2017), while the last
three columns capture the analysis conducted using the growth rates observed
between 2008 and 2017.

Table 6.3 reveals that, as expected, firm effects are the strongest ones and
account for almost two-thirds of the variance. More interestingly, the impact
of BM outweighs the effect of the industry, providing substantial support
for the assumption that BMs are associated with significant variance in firm
performance. If we consider the annual performance, the BM effect ranges

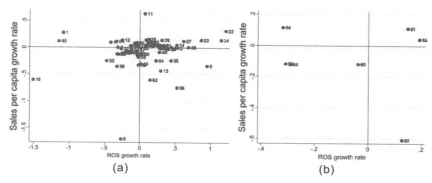

Note: For each BM, the sales per capita (ROS) growth rate is computed as the median value of the sales per capita (ROS) growth rates between 2008 and 2017 of the firms included in the BM.

Figure 6.3   *Map of the business models based on the growth rates on sales per capita and ROS: panel (a) All industries; panel (b) Industry NACE code: 2229*

Table 6.3   *Percentage of variance accounted by firm, BM and industry level – Multilevel mixed-effects linear regressions*

Variable	Annual values for the period 2009–2017			Growth rates between 2008 and 2017		
	Firm	BM	Industry	Firm	BM	Industry
Value added per capita	76.323	23.676	0.001	65.090	30.569	4.341
Sales per capita	72.140	27.860	0.000	66.803	31.480	1.717
ROS	64.875	35.110	0.015	81.305	14.226	4.469
ROA	68.491	31.497	0.012	81.017	15.547	3.436
ROI	71.059	22.476	6.465	79.408	12.917	7.675

Notes: N=14040 (1560*9) for the annual values and 1560 for the growth rates.

from 22.5 per cent (ROI) to 35.1 per cent (ROS), while, for the performance growth rates, the BM effect varies between 12.9 per cent (ROI) and 31.5 per cent (sales per capita) With regard to the industry, its effects on performance levels are negligible (except in the case of the ROI). It should be noted that the industry effects are stronger when we consider the performance growth rates; specifically, the industry effect ranges from 1.7 per cent (ROI) to 7.7 per cent (sales per capita), but it is always lower than the BM effect.

5.   CONCLUSIONS

This chapter analyses the effects of BMs on firm performance and disentangles them from the impact of the industry and firm levels. By clustering financial statement information for Italian SMEs operating in nine manufacturing industries, we build a taxonomy of intra-industry BMs. These BMs show different dynamics in terms of performance, and we observe both growing and declining BMs. We also find significant differences between the considered indicators of performance. After mapping the BMs in four quadrants on the basis of their dynamics in terms of value creation (sales per capita growth between 2008–2017) and value capture (ROS growth between 2008–2017), we see that our previously identified (65) BMs are distributed across all the quadrants. Finally, we decompose the total variability of several measures of performance into three parts to determine the relative role of BM with respect to both the industry and the firm-level effects. The results show that the BM effects outweigh the industry effects, and account, on average, for one-third of the observed total variance.

The main contribution of this chapter is twofold: first, we provide empirical evidence that BMs, which are regarded as a distinct element of the system shaping firm performance, play a relevant role in explaining the heterogeneity in firm performance across industries. Second, we provide a methodology aimed at properly identifying firm BMs. Because of the difficulties lying in the definition and measurement of the key elements of BMs, most of the existing literature resorts to case studies or focuses on a single industry. This work thus demonstrates that financial statement data can be used to classify firms into BMs. The usefulness of the proposed methodology is strengthened by its ease of adoption and by the large availability of data on corporate financial statements.

At the same time, this study inevitably presents some limitations. For instance, due to the complexities involved, we do not answer more in-depth inquiries concerning which combination of BM-related characteristics is the most important in predicting firm performance; also, we only marginally consider the effects of business model changes on firm performance. These issues may be addressed by future research.

REFERENCES

Afuah, A. (2004), *Business Models: A Strategic Management Approach*. Irwin/ McGraw-Hill, New York, NY.
Afuah, A. and Tucci, C.L. (2001), *Internet Business Models and Strategies: Text and Cases*. McGraw-Hill, New York, NY.
Amit, R. and Zott, C. (2012), Creating value through business model innovation. *MIT Sloan Management Review*, 53(3), pp. 41–49.
Andersen, J. (2011), Strategic resources and firm performance. *Management Decision*, 49(1), pp. 87–98.

Barney, J. (1991), Firm resources and sustained competitive advantage. *Journal of Management*, 17, pp. 99–120.

Bigliardi, B., Nosella, A. and Verbano, C. (2005), Business models in Italian biotechnology industry: A quantitative analysis. *Technovation*, 25, pp. 1299–1306.

Bryk, A.S. and Raudenbush, S.W. (1992), *Hierarchical Linear Models: Applications and Data Analysis Methods*. Sage, Newbury Park, CA.

Casadesus-Masanell, R. and Ricart, J.E. (2011), How to design a winning business model. *Harvard Business Review*, 89(1–2), pp. 100–107.

DeYoung, R. (2005), The performance of internet-based business models: Evidence from the banking industry. *Journal of Business*, 78(3), pp. 893–947.

Glick, J.L. (2008), Biotechnology business models work: Evidence from the pharmaceutical marketplace. *Journal of Commercial Biotechnology*, 14, pp. 106–117.

Lanzolla, G. and Markides, C. (2021), A business model view of strategy. *Journal of Management Studies*, 58(2), pp. 540–553.

Magretta, J. (2002), Why business models matter. *Harvard Business Review*, 80(5), pp. 86–92.

Malone, T., Weill, P., Lai, R., D'Urso, V., Herman, G., Apel, T. and Woerner, S. (2006), Do some business models perform better than others? MPRA Paper 4751, University Library of Munich, Germany.

McGahan, A.M. and Porter, M.E. (1997), How much does industry matter, really? *Strategic Management Journal*, 18, pp. 15–30.

Mehmetoglu, M. and Jakobsen, T.G. (2017), *Applied Statistics Using Stata: A Guide for the Social Sciences*. Sage, Thousand Oaks, CA.

Morris, M., Schindehutte, M. and Allen, J. (2006), The entrepreneur's business model: Toward a unified perspective. *Journal of Business Research*, 58(6), pp. 726–735.

Morris, M.H., Shirokova, G. and Shatalov, A. (2013), The business model and firm performance: The case of Russian food service ventures. *Journal of Small Business Management*, 51(1), pp. 46–65.

Nair, S., Nisar, A., Palacios, M. and Ruiz, F. (2012), Impact of knowledge brokering on performance heterogeneity among business models. *Management Decision*, 50(9), pp. 1649–1660.

Porter, M.E. (1985) How information gives you competitive advantage. *Harvard Business Review*, 63(4), pp. 149–160.

Rumelt, R.P. (1991), How much does industry matter? *Strategic Management Journal*, 12(3), pp. 167–185.

Sabatier, V., Mangematin, V. and Rousselle, T. (2010). From recipe to dinner: Business model portfolios in the European bio-pharmaceutical industry. *Long Range Planning*, 43, pp. 431–447.

Velu, C. (2015), The effects of the degree of business model innovation and third-party alliance on the survival of new firms. *Technovation*, 35, pp. 1–11.

Verdin, P. and Tackx, K. (2015), Are you creating or capturing value? A dynamic framework for sustainable strategy. *M-RCBG Working Paper Series*, 36, pp. 1–19.

Wernerfelt, B. (1984), A resource-based view of the firm. *Strategic Management Journal*, 5(2), pp. 171–180.

Wirtz, B.W., Pistoia, A., Ullrich, S. and Göttel, V. (2016), Business models: Origin, development and future research perspectives. *Long Range Planning*, 49(1), pp. 36–54.

Zott, C. and Amit, R. (2007), Business model design and the performance of entrepreneurial firms. *Organization Science*, 18, pp. 181–199.

Zott, C., and Amit, R.H. (2008), The fit between product market strategy and business model: Implications for firm performance. *Strategic Management Journal*, 29(1), pp. 1–26.

Zott, C., Amit, R. and Massa, L. (2011), The business model: Recent developments and future research. *Journal of Management*, 37(4), pp. 1019–1042.

7. Identifying business models with the use of metadata

Jasmine Mondolo and Marco Cucculelli

1. INTRODUCTION

The manufacturing industry, which has long played an important role in the European economy (see Eurostat, 2021, for an overview), has recently undergone relevant changes mainly driven by globalization and technological change. Countries have indeed become more and more interconnected, with increasing flows of trade and foreign direct investment. In the meantime, the latest wave of technological progress, driven by the spread of new digital technologies and innovative organizational practices, has displayed unprecedented pace and pervasiveness (Staccioli & Virgillito, 2021).

Firms' ability to cope with such a dynamic and competitive setting strongly hinges upon their distinctive set of tangible and intangible assets, which, according to the Resource-Based View, are an important source of competitive advantage (Barney, 1991), and shape the firm's business model. Hence, companies need to be adequately aware of their own resources and capabilities; at the same time, they are also expected to sufficiently know the business model, and thus the competencies, strategies and actions of other relevant players, such as their actual and potential competitors and partners (Kronemeyer et al., 2021). Indeed, part of a firm's success and performance depends on the firm's context, and in particular to the cluster to which it belongs. Notably, clusters typically foster learning and innovation across different organizational settings and boundaries (Papagiannidis et al., 2018). As key enabling technologies require increasing complexity of collaboration and networking, in recent years clusters have become even more important for boosting the spread of innovation and distributing the risks and costs associated with emerging technological developments (Assimakopoulos et al., 2015).

An appropriate assessment of firms' business models requires detailed information on these subjects' resources, capabilities and strategies. This information can be gathered through surveys, whose implementation, however, requires considerable effort, resources and time. In recent years, technological progress has equipped researchers with emerging web crawler technologies and real-time big data, which can offer valuable support in this respect (Papagiannidis et al., 2018). Accordingly, an increasing number of studies have resorted to these alternative sources, and in particular to firms' websites, to detect companies' activities, business models, industrial clusters or collaborative networks (e.g., Libaers et al., 2010; Arora et al., 2013; Nathan & Rosso, 2015; Marra et al., 2015; Marra et al., 2020). Nonetheless, so far, most studies have identified firms' specializations and commonalities starting from their activity as defined by standard industrial classifications (SICs), such as NACE (the statistical classification of economic activities in the European Community) and NAICS (the North American Industry Classification System), which are based on a top-down approach and present several drawbacks. For instance, the level of detail is too coarse for differentiating activities that are similar, but not the same (Cortright & Mayer, 2001); also, conventional classifications are too rigid to properly account for the changeable and rapidly growing range of new technologies, solutions, products, and services (Nathan & Rosso, 2015); furthermore, real-world features of businesses in an industry tend to evolve ahead of any given industrial categorization (Fan & Lang, 2000).

In this chapter, we aim to provide a more realistic and updated representation of what companies are and what they do, and to show how clusters can be identified, based on firms' business model similarities, starting from the analysis of their products, technologies, know-how and other BM-related characteristics. To this purpose, we put forward a bottom-up approach which, using text-mining techniques, elicits detailed corporate information from the companies' websites. The content of these websites, which firms use to present their profile, products and services, can help to shed light on the firms' technologies, achievements, key marketing decisions, strategies, relationships with stakeholders and domain, and, accordingly, their business model (Gök et al., 2015; Stathoulopoulos & Mateos-Garcia, 2017). The keywords and terms that store this information are defined as metadata or tags. Through a network analysis, we use these tags to link companies according to their BM analogies, and in doing so, to detect clusters. We apply this methodology to a group of firms located in a small-sized NUT-2 region of Central Italy, the Marche, whose industrial landscape is characterized by a large amount of manufacturing small- and medium-sized enterprises (SMEs) that often belong to industrial districts.

From the application of our three-step procedure, it emerges that the selected companies form five clusters, also known as communities, which are driven by their complementarities in terms of business model. In doing so, we propose a method that can help firms attain a better understanding of their competitive environment, which in turn can improve corporate decision-making, including decisions about partnerships and supply chain integration (Flynn et al., 2010).

This approach may also be employed by researchers who intend to perform an accurate assessment of firms' specificities and complementarities on different and maybe larger samples.

The balance of this chapter is organized as follows. Section 2 briefly depicts the conceptual framework and reviews the pertinent literature. Section 3 presents the data and the methodology. Section 4 applies the three-step procedure to the selected sample of firms and provides some preliminary figures. Section 5 describes the five communities into which manufacturing firms cluster. Finally, Section 6 concludes.

2.   CONCEPTUAL FRAMEWORK AND LITERATURE REVIEW

In the economics literature, the study of firms' characteristics, boundaries and dynamics has been conducted using different perspectives. According to the classical model of Industrial Organization Economics, the so-called Structure-Conduct-Performance (SCP) paradigm or model, the only prerequisite for differentiating companies within the industry is the firm's scale of operation (Matyjas, 2014). Hence, firms are all seen as strictly homogeneous from the point of view of their strategies, and their behaviour or conduct is determined by the industry structure. In recent years, the SCP approach has been subjected to widespread criticism. Its main limitation is that it provides a poor (and even misleading) basis for policy formulation, because it fails to address, not to mention opening, the 'black box' of the firm role (Barney, 2001).

The assumption of firm homogeneity, which is integral to the SCP paradigm, is rejected by the Resource-Based View (RBV, also known as Resource-Based Theory). The RBV sees companies as collectors of resources and capabilities, which allow them to be competitive in the market (Powell, 2001). Consequently, the most profitable firms are those that possess resources and/or internal capabilities which are somehow better than those of their competitors (Hitt et al., 2002). Furthermore, profitability is not defined by the company's industrial sector (Grant, 1995). According to the Resource-Based theory, the resources and competencies owned by enterprises in the same industry are often very different from each other (Barney, 1991); in other words, they vary not only across sectors, but also across firms within the same industry, which, consequently, operate in different ways (Peteraf, 1993; Mills et al., 2002).

The analysis of the capabilities and competencies of a firm is then central to the accurate identification and analysis of its business strategy and identity (Milara, 2014) and, in turn, its business model. For this reason, some researchers and organizations have gathered information from the Internet, and in particular from the firms' websites, in order to analyse firms' activities, detect industrial clusters, identify collaborative networks and so on. To give a few examples, Libaers et al. (2010) resort to exploratory factor analysis of keyword occurrence on firm websites to build a taxonomy of business models used by small, highly innovative firms focused on technology commercialization. Arora et al. (2013) perform a web content analysis to examine the activities of SMEs located in the US, UK and China and commercializing emerging graphene technologies. Nathan & Rosso (2015) combine UK administrative microdata, media and website content to develop experimental measures of firm innovation for SMEs. Stathoulopoulos & Mateos-Garcia (2017) propose a system based on open data that enables the exploration of the digital and tech company space with high granularity through keywords, specific technologies and company names, as well as to create thematic topics characterising these companies' activities. Also, Heroux-Vaillancourt, Beaudry et al. (2016) explore the use of web content analysis to build innovation indicators from the complete texts of 79 corporate websites of Canadian nanotechnology and advanced materials firms.

Some studies that employ text data attempt to complement and improve standard business classifications. As an illustration, Gök et al. (2014) resort to commercial company directories and keyword-based search to define a 'Green product' group of organizations, thus introducing a new code; Shapira et al. (2011) examine the trends in nanotechnology using a similar approach. Also, Gök et al. (2015) apply a keyword technique to explore the R&D activities of 296 UK-based green-good SMEs, and find that website data offer additional insights compared to other traditional unobtrusive research methods, such as patent and publication analysis. Finally, Papagiannidis et al. (2018), who highlight the limitations of SIC codes, put forward a new big-data-mining methodology for industry classification and cluster detection.

Furthermore, a few contributions resort to metadata to identify firms' specializations, industrial clusters and technological or market complementarities in high-tech sectors. For instance, Marra et al. (2015) and Marra et al. (2017) apply a network analysis on tags collected by CrunchBase to detect firm specializations, market and technological complementarities in the green-tech sector and the software sector, respectively. Additionally, Marra et al. (2020) apply network analysis to metadata for the main purpose of providing firms that look for collaborations and knowledge exchanges with methodological support for the screening of potential partners.

Our work ties particularly well to the study by Papagiannidis et al. (2018), from which it differs in the following main respects: it performs a different type of data analysis, which can be easily handled also by economic researchers who do not possess specific skills in informatics and data science; it identifies clusters based on business model similarities; it provides a descriptive overview for each of the identified communities that highlights the prevailing business model-related features and economic performance, and that facilitates comparisons across clusters; it considers a sample of manufacturing firms located in a small Italian NUTS-2 region (the Marche) where the presence of manufacturing SMEs grouped into industrial districts is a distinctive feature of the local production system; thus, this context can be particularly suitable for this type of analysis.

3.   DATA AND METHODOLOGY

In this study, we consider a sample of manufacturing enterprises located in the Marche and registered in the Bureau Van Dijk's Aida database, which covers more than 500,000 Italian limited liability companies. The data employed in the main analysis refer to the year 2018; in Section 4, information on three firm-level indicators is provided for the years 2009–2017 as well. Starting from a sample of about 18,000 manufacturing companies, we single out a subset of 244 firms following two criteria, namely, a minimum revenue threshold of 10 million euro and the availability of the website URL. Then, we implement a method which encompasses three main subsequent phases, namely, Web Content Mining, Network Analysis, and Reorganization and Ranking of the Metadata. A brief illustration of each of these stages is provided below.

Phase 1: Web Content Mining

Starting from the list of the firms' website URLs, we first conduct a web scraping process through the software Nutch (Cafarella & Cutting, 2004). Nutch is a highly extensible and scalable open-source web crawler that fetches, parses and indexes a list of URLs while complying with a series of constraints. The final result of Phase 1 consists in a document/term matrix (i.e., a mathematical matrix which describes the frequency of terms that occur in a collection of documents), where the rows represent the companies (the terms), the columns refer to the metadata (the documents), and the intersections indicate whether a certain tag is present in a certain website.

Phase 2: Network Analysis

In the second step, we investigate the relationships between companies, which are based on commonalities and complementarities in terms of business models. For this purpose, we resort to the tool of the network analysis. Specifically, we build a network of companies, where the latter are the nodes, and a link exists between two companies if the latter have at least one tag in common (namely, if they specialize in the same or similar products, services and technologies). Linkages in the network are weighted by the number of shared tags, so the weight of a link between two companies is heavier the larger the number of tags these firms have in common (or, in other words, the higher the similarities/complementarities in terms of business model).

We perform the network analysis via the open-source software Gephi (Bastian et al., 2009), which makes it possible to compute the most common network metrics. The one that better serves our purpose is modularity; modularity is designed to measure the strength of a network division into communities, which are also called groups, clusters or modules. A community can be defined as a group of nodes with dense internal connections (cohesion) and weak external relationships (separation) with nodes of other groups. A popular method for community detection is the one devised by Blondel et al. (2008). This approach, which is also referred to as the Louvain method, maximizes a modularity score for each community; it has several advantages, such as easy implementation, fast computation speed, and the capability to handle large and weighted networks. More importantly, it turned out that, compared to other methods, Blondel's algorithm provides higher-quality results for community detection (Pons and Latapy, 2006; Lancichinetti and Fortunato, 2009).

Phase 3: Reorganization and Ranking of the Metadata

The last stage of our analysis consists in the reorganization and ranking of the metadata based on the information on modularity retrieved in the previous phase. It should be noticed that a tag shared by two companies belonging to the same community (each of which displays a certain modularity score) cannot be directly assigned to that community, and a rearrangement is required. Indeed, it is possible that two firms are linked (on the basis of their metadata) even if they belong to two distinct communities; accordingly, we have to account for this possible circumstance.

The following example helps clarify this point: looking at Table 7.1, we can see that tags B and F belong to Company α and Company Ω and that, in both cases, the modularity class is 'two'; on the other hand, tag D belongs to both Company β and Company Ω even though the former is in the community with modularity class 'one' and the latter is in the community with modularity class 'two'.

Finally, we assign a score and then rank the tags according to their clustering tendency, that is, the degree to which the data contain an inherent grouping structure. The clustering tendency is calculated as the product of the distribution factor (the metadata occurrence frequency among communities) and the weight factor (the metadata occurrence frequency within each community). At the end of Phase 3, we obtain a set of communities by looking at the ranking of the related metadata.

Table 7.1   Metadata by company and modularity class (example)

Name	Community (modularity class)	Metadata
Company α	2	B,F
Company β	1	A,C,D,E,
...	...	...
...	...	...
Company Ω	2	B,D,F

4.   APPLICATION OF THE PROPOSED APPROACH

We apply the approach shortly described in Section 3 to the selected sample of manufacturing firms. First, using the software Nutch, we crawl the firms' websites and extract information on their competencies, markets and activities. In doing so, we obtain about 9,000 words contained in 1,189 web pages from the 244 sampled websites. Then, after removing the 'stop words' (i.e., words that are very commonly used in a given language, and thus are not very informative) and merging synonyms, we end up with 2,726 tags (corresponding to 1,270 unique words), with an average of 11 tags per firm.

Next, we use the previously selected companies and the metadata collected in Phase 1 to conduct the network analysis of Phase 2. The network of firms resulting from the co-occurrence of metadata consists of 244 nodes (representing the sampled manufacturing companies) and 10,429 edges. Edges are undirected and weighted, and capture firms' commonalities and complementarities in terms of products, knowledge, skills and attitudes. In other words, two firms are linked if they specialize in the same products, markets, technologies, and thus rely on similar business models; accordingly, the level of interconnection can be regarded as a proxy of firms' BM complementarities, which in turn can foster cooperation (Marra et al. 2017).

Some useful information about this network is provided in Table 7.2, which condenses some relevant network statistics. One of the most popular network metrics is density, which measures the share of realized links over the number of all possible links. A density of 0.35 means that 35 per cent of all possible edges are realized or, in other words, that, taking two nodes at random, the probability that they are connected through an edge equals 35 per cent. Typically, the higher the magnitude of the network, the lower the density; in addition, density tends to be higher in the case of undirected networks where relationships are not formal or (as in this case) are based on similarities between nodes. Another important indicator is the average network degree (i.e., the average number of edges attached to a node), which in this

Table 7.2   Main network metrics

Metrics	Value
Number of nodes	244
Number of edges	10,429
Avg. degree	85.4
Avg. weighted degree	121.3
Network diameter	9
Avg. path length	2.9
Density	0.35
Modularity	0.48
Avg. clustering coefficient	0.72

Source: Authors' elaboration of CrunchBase data.

network equals 85.4, implying that, on average, a node is connected through a link to about 85 nodes; considering the magnitude of the network, we can posit that this value can be regarded as quite high. The average shortest path length indicates that the average (topological) distance between two firms is about 3; this value is lower than half of the diameter, according to which the distance between the two most remote firms of the network (that is, the two most different firms in terms of business model) equals 9; hence, the average path length can be regarded as quite short.

Finally, modularity and the average clustering coefficient are two relevant cluster-level metrics that provide information about the tendency to clustering of a network. Specifically, the average clustering coefficient is the average of all the node-level local clustering coefficients, which capture the percentage of realized links between the alters of a node (i.e., between the nodes that are linked through an edge to a certain node). An average clustering coefficient of 0.72 means that, on average, 72 per cent of all the possible links between a node's alters are realized. Modularity captures the extent to which the nodes of a network tend to group into clusters or communities, and ranges from 0 to 1. A value of 0.48 can be regarded as moderate. A more in-depth analysis of modularity reveals that the network structure is characterized by five main aggregates or communities, as we will better clarify later.

With regard to Phase 3, after ranking the sets of metadata, we classify them into three different BM-related categories, that is, business orientation, organizational aspects of business, and technical know-how. Subsequently, using the above-mentioned categories, we identify five relevant communities, which are briefly illustrated in Section 5.

5.   AN OVERVIEW OF THE FIVE COMMUNITIES

The final output of the approach described in Section 3 is the clustering of manufacturing firms into five communities, which differ in terms of number of firms, sectors involved, BM-related characteristics (i.e., business orientation, know-how and organizational aspects), average firm size and economic performance. A description of each of these communities is provided below.

Community 'Modularity System-based' (Community 0)

The first community can be labelled 'modularity system-based' and refers to manufacturing businesses (corresponding to about 21 per cent of the sampled companies) characterized by organizational aspects such as supply-chain integration, personalization and flexibility (Table 7.3). The know-how includes wood processing and chemistry (plastic materials). Most of the firms belonging to this community manufacture low- or medium-technology products, such as footwear components (e.g., heels, stays, shanks, counters) and furniture systems (i.e., modules and connectors). These production types, which are sometimes referred to as modular production systems and modular manufacturing systems, present extreme internal flexibility and make use of modularization (i.e., the activity of dividing a product or system into interchangeable modules). As a result, they are able to perform a wide range of functions, products and services, and can be easily personalized and/or reorganized in the face of the changeable conditions of supply chains. In this regard, the manufacturing businesses under scrutiny no longer compete solely as autonomous corporations, but also as participants in integrated supply chains. Within supply chains, strategic partnerships can be beneficial to the various actors (generating a win-win situation). In this competitive and dynamic context, the success of a firm increasingly depends on the management's ability to integrate the company's networks of business relationships and update products that meet their markets, thus ensuring the supply chain evolves accordingly. For these reasons, such businesses are often engaged in product innovation and display a high degree of export orientation.

Table 7.3 condenses some community-level indicators of economic performance for the period 2009–2018. For instance, we can notice that the average firm size (145.6 employees) is not negligible. This result can seem at odds with the fact that most of the Italian manufacturing firms are small-sized; however, it is consistent with the selection criteria we applied at the beginning of the procedure. Further, the profitability indexes present strong variability within the sample. For instance, the Return on Assets (ROA), which, on average, amounts to 3.7 per cent, ranges between -64.4 and 12.5 per cent, with negative values indicating an operating loss.

Table 7.3 Community 0 'modularity system-based'

METADATA				
Business orientation		design		
		export		
		product innovation		
Organizational aspects		supply chain integration		
		flexibility		
		personalization		
Know-how		chemistry – plastics		
		wood and derivatives		
Sectors involved		footwear components		
		furnishing systems and components		
PERFORMANCE				
Variable	Min	Max	Mean	Std. Dev.
employees	19.1	1,484.4	145.6	31.2
revenues (Thsnd EUR)	8,053.7	317,265.3	31,527.0	8,832.7
ROE (%)	-61.1	25.6	5.8	3.3
ROI (%)	-15.0	24.5	8.3	4.2
ROA (%)	-64.4	12.5	3.7	1.7
ROS (%)	-14.1	13.1	4.0	2.2
EBITDA to sales	-41.7	16.9	7.1	2.6

Source: Authors' elaboration of AIDA and CrunchBase data.

Community 'Engineering Designers' (Community 1)

The 'Engineering designers' community corresponds to the largest share of sampled firms (27 per cent). It refers to businesses whose manufacturing processes present high levels of technological content and product quality, and especially of customization and automation use (Table 7.4). The metalworking and the transport equipment sectors are the most represented ones in this cluster, followed by the machinery and the printing industries. Companies rely on a strong technical background and knowledge coupled with engineering capabilities to design, create and produce technical solutions according to customers' requirements; innovation efforts are mainly directed at process improvements. Two major activities carried out by these firms are rapid prototyping and batch manufacturing. In this context, 3D printing technology is a widely known and adopted automation technology which, starting from

Table 7.4   Community 1 'Engineering designers'

METADATA				
Business orientation	engineering			
	client focused			
	process innovation			
Organizational aspects	prototyping			
	automation			
	batch manufacturing			
Know-how	steel – aluminium			
	Software/CNC/CAD/CAM/3D			
Sectors involved	Industrial components (automotive/household appliance)			
	metalworking industry			
PERFORMANCE				
Variable	Min	Max	Mean	Std. Dev.
employees	9.3	1,291.3	133.4	29.8
revenues (Thsnd EUR)	7,367.9	380,159.0	32,214.1	7,093.2
ROE (%)	-22.3	38.7	11.2	3.8
ROI (%)	-2.1	24.8	10.1	1.3
ROA (%)	-6.1	34.9	6.3	2.9
ROS (%)	-2.4	18.3	5.3	2.1
EBITDA to sales	1.7		8.9	3.2

Source: Authors' elaboration of AIDA and CrunchBase data.

materials such as steel and aluminium, boosts opportunities for one-piece productions that can be crafted and delivered within ever-shortening time frames. Other widespread advanced technologies are CNC manufacturing (a computerized manufacturing process in which pre-programmed software and code control the movement of production equipment), as well as CAD and CAM models. CAD/CAM applications are used for both designing a product and programming the manufacturing processes; the CNC system determines the processes necessary to machine raw material (e.g., aluminium, steel and titanium) into finished parts; it guarantees great machining accuracy, as the entire process is run through automation of tasks.

Table 7.4 reports some community-level indicators of economic performance for the period 2009–2018. Also in this community, the average firm size is considerable (133 employees), and the profitability indexes present strong variability within the sample. For example, the mean value of the EBITDA to sales ratio is 8.9% per cent, ranging between 1.7 and 29.8 per cent.

Community 'Human Capital-based' (Community 2)

The so-called 'Human capital-based' community, which is the smallest one in terms of the share of sampled companies it covers (16 per cent), refers to manufacturing businesses characterized by a rich and long tradition based on consolidated expertise and competencies that are passed from one generation to another (Table 7.5). These companies often operate in fashion-related industries (e.g., textile, clothing and footwear, and accessories), and in the wine industry as well. They heavily rely on manual tasks carried out by a skilled labour force in order to realize home-made, high-quality products and perform quality control. Accordingly, human capital plays a central role within this cluster. The so-called 'Made in Italy' hallmark of these companies mirrors an entrepreneurial culture based on a set of distinctive features, such as consistent quality delivery, craftsmanship, recognizable style and design, unique taste, exclusivity, emotional appeal, global brand reputation and presence of elements of uniqueness. Even though the production employs quite simple raw materials, like leather and cloth fabric, the material processing, which is essential to ensuring the quality of finished products, is challenging. Moreover, in recent years, the increasing adoption of advanced technologies has called for better technical and digital skills. These skills assist manufacturers in production planning, production control and online monitoring, and to help them make good, long-sighted choices about the suppliers of raw materials.

In this community, like in Community 0, firms are strongly export-oriented. Additionally, they tend to use the Internet, websites, social media and e-commerce platforms in order to reach foreign markets and reinforce their relationship with their customers. In particular, they resort to social media channels mainly to encourage brand experience. Concerning their websites, while some companies possess websites that allow users to make orders, but the latter are forwarded to local suppliers and shops, others adopt a complete e-commerce system; hence, users can find the whole product portfolio both online and offline.

Community 'Eco-friendly' (Community 3)

The fourth community, labelled 'Eco-friendly', is made up of companies (19 per cent of the sample) that define their strategies and operations paying particular attention to sustainability. Hence, they manufacture products through economically sound processes that minimize negative environmental impacts (Table 7.6). Similar to those belonging to the 'human capital-based' community, firms are often exporters, and use e-commerce platforms to engage with customers and to extend their access to foreign markets. Also, they resort to quite specialized labour employed in automated and personalized production

Table 7.5   *Community 2 'Human capital-based'*

METADATA				
Business orientation		export		
		tradition		
		made in Italy		
Organizational aspects		craftmanship		
		quality control		
		e-commerce		
		social media		
Know-how		leather		
		textiles		
Sectors involved		fashion		
		footwear and accessories		
		wine industry		
PERFORMANCE				
Variable	Min	Max	Mean	Std. Dev.
employees	14.3	1,641.7	153.0	34.5
revenues (Thsnd EUR)	8,388.9	642,616.6	40,023.1	5,753.8
ROE (%)	-13.0	31.3	8.3	2.0
ROI (%)	-8.8	27.1	8.6	1.9
ROA (%)	-13.0	26.5	5.2	3.7
ROS (%)	-6.6	19.1	4.7	1.6
EBITDA to sales	-17.6	23.0	7.0	2.5

Source: Authors' elaboration of AIDA and CrunchBase data.

processes, and the results are often patented. The main fields of knowledge include chemistry and the study of the properties of materials (mainly plastic materials and paper). Additive Manufacturing (AM) technologies are exploited as well. In particular, AM technologies allow companies to develop and manufacture complex parts and functional products with a high level of customization. Examples of firms that can effectively grasp the benefits of AM are those in the packaging sector. Some of the latest advances in AM have increased the versatility of these firms by allowing them to conduct blow-moulding processes, realize hollow prototypes of great complexity, work with a full range of packaging materials, use thermoforming to create prototypes of trays and blister packs, and much more. Accordingly, many firms belonging to this community operate in the packaging industry.

Some relevant indicators of economic performance referring to the 'Eco-friendly' community are presented in Table 7.6. Firms are, on average,

Table 7.6   *Community 3 'Eco friendly'*

METADATA				
Business orientation		sustainability		
		export		
		patenting		
Organizational aspects		automation		
		personalization		
		e-commerce		
		after-sales service		
Know-how		chemistry – plastics materials		
		paper		
		additive manufacturing		
Sectors involved		packaging		
PERFORMANCE				
Variable	Min	Max	Mean	Std. Dev.
employees	13.2	1,123.6	129.3	21.8
revenues (Thsnd EUR)	8,649.0	420,257.2	39,770.5	7,423.8
ROE (%)	-3.5	61.0	11.9	1.0
ROI (%)	-5.3	28.3	10.5	1.5
ROA (%)	1.1	28.9	7.5	2.2
ROS (%)	-0.5	26.9	6.4	2.1
EBITDA to sales	2.4	35.5	10.6	1.6

Source: Authors' elaboration of AIDA and CrunchBase data.

smaller than the manufacturing firms belonging to the other clusters, with a mean number of employees of 129. Additionally, the average Return on Equity (ROE) and the average Return on Investment (ROI), which equal 11.9 per cent and 10.5 per cent respectively, are higher than the average values reported for other communities.

Community 'Certified Business' (Community 4)

The 'Certified business' community, which covers 17 per cent of the selected firms, is the most heterogeneous one in terms of sectoral coverage. In particular, it involves both the food industry and the construction industry (Table 7.7). A common element of the firms belonging to this community and working in different sectors is that their activities and outputs can considerably affect their customers' health and safety. Accordingly, they typically must comply with a number of complex regulations when making and selling products, and they are often motivated to acquire environmental or quality certifications. Quality certification contributes to demonstrating that the organization of these manufacturing businesses is customer-focused and committed to delivering consistent, high-quality products; the environmental certification helps firms quantify, monitor and control the ongoing environmental impact of their operations. For example, by managing the use of natural resources, energy and waste, these companies improve their corporate image and credibility, reach new customers and identify opportunities for cost savings.

The companies belonging to this community rely on very different competencies, which also vary according to the sector; despite that, all of them generally master blockchain technologies. Blockchain applications for companies in the construction industry are mainly related to contract management, the Building Information Modelling (BIM) system, supply chain management and funding management. Instead, companies in the food industry exploit blockchain applications to detect product alterations, identify contaminated products and increase consumers' trust in the producers and distributors. The data enclosed in the blockchains can indeed be shared across multiple parties, thus enhancing a transparent process.

To further illustrate the 'Certified business' community, some major indicators of economic performance are reported in Table 7.7. We can see that companies in the community are, on average, larger than the firms belonging to the other clusters, with a mean number of employees of 180. Firms also achieve a higher average sales revenue (47 thousand euro), whereas the average ROE and the average ROI are lower (5.7 per cent and 7 per cent respectively).

To sum up, the identified communities are quite heterogeneous regarding, for instance, the sectors involved, business models, average firm size and economic performance. For instance, the average firm size (which, as previously mentioned, is influenced by the criteria used for the sample selection) varies from 129 (Community 3) to 180 (Community 4). Moreover, the average revenue from sales ranges from about 30 thousand euro (Community 0) to 50 thousand euro (Community 4); the ROA is between 3.7 per cent (Community 0) and 7.5 per cent (Community 3), while the EBITDA to sales ratio ranges from 7 per cent (Community 2) to 10.6 per cent (Community 3).

6.   CONCLUSIONS

The manufacturing industry has recently experienced major changes, mainly driven by globalization and technological advances, and is expected to further evolve. In this dynamic and competitive environment, companies' success increasingly depends on their inner resources, competencies and capabilities – which shape the firm's business model – but also on those of their competitors and their potential partners. In order to attain a sound assessment of the

Table 7.7   Community 4 'Certified business'

METADATA				
Business orientation		environmental/quality certification		
		client focused		
		export		
Organizational aspects		copacker (GDO)		
		e-commerce		
Know-how		blockchain technologies		
Sectors involved		food		
		catering industry		
		construction		
PERFORMANCE				
Variable	Min	Max	Mean	Std. Dev.
employees	14.7	1.470,2	180.7	19.1
revenues (Thsnd EUR)	9,399.8	272,820.8	47,089.1	8,297.1
ROE (%)	-40.2	26.5	5.7	1.3
ROI (%)	-11.4	24.3	7.0	2.0
ROA (%)	-12.4	17.3	4.8	1.7
ROS (%)	-18.6	24.1	4.1	1.1
EBITDA to sales	-10.1	29.6	7.1	2.4

Source: Authors' elaboration of AIDA and CrunchBase data.

companies' business models, and also to group them into clusters based on business model similarities, detailed information on these subjects is required. While the use of standard industrial classifications for identifying firms' activities presents several limitations, the analysis of the Internet, and especially of firms' websites, can be particularly helpful in this respect.

In light of these considerations, we propose a bottom-up approach which exploits detailed information on firms' specializations, competencies and skills retrieved from the companies' websites. We apply this methodology to a sample of manufacturing firms located in a small Italian NUTS-2 region, the Marche, whose productive system is characterized by the significant presence of manufacturing firms that tend to operate in industrial districts. In doing so, we identify five relevant communities or clusters (i.e., modularity system-based, engineering designers, human capital-based, eco-friendly and certified business), each of which encompasses various traditionally defined sectors, presents a number of peculiar business model features, and exhibits a certain average economic performance. We thus provide an evidence-based picture of firms' activities based on the business orientation, products, know-how and organizational aspects to which manufacturing firms de facto direct their efforts.

The proposed method can help firms to identify and better understand their actual or potential competitors and partners. It can also support researchers who intend to identify clusters without resorting to standard industrial classifications. Finally, this approach, which hinges upon firms' specificities and accounts for within-sector heterogeneity, may contribute to defining more specific and targeted policy interventions. For example, a local government may decide to support the firms involved in the supply chain of a certain product or belonging to a given cluster rather than indistinctly consider all the firms that are labelled with a certain SIC code. Future research may attempt to apply the proposed analysis to other territories and sectors in order to test the robustness of this methodology and to produce a more systematic and large-scale classification of businesses that goes beyond SICs. In addition, taking advantage of the ability of the Internet to produce dynamic and updated streams of data, researchers may analyse how industrial clusters, along with firms' business models, evolve over time.

REFERENCES

Arora, S.K., Youtie, J., Shapira, P., Gao, L. & Ma, T.T. (2013). Entry strategies in an emerging technology: A pilot web-based study of graphene firms. *Scientometrics*, 95(3), pp. 1189–1207.

Assimakopoulos, D.G., Oshri, I. & Pandza, K. (2015). *Management of Emerging Technologies for Socio-Economic Impact*. Cheltenham: Edward Elgar Publishing.

Barney, J.B. (1991). Firm resources and sustained competitive advantage. *Journal of Management*, 17, pp. 99–119.

Barney, J.B. (2001). Is the resource-based 'view' a useful perspective for strategic management research? Yes. *Academy of Management Review*, 26(1), pp. 41–56.

Bastian, M., Heymann, S. & Jacomy, M. (2009). Gephi: An open source software for exploring and manipulating networks. In Third International AAAI Conference on Weblogs and Social Media.

Blondel, V.D., Guillaume, J.-L., Lambiotte, R. & Lefebvre, E. (2008). Fast unfolding of communities in large networks. *Journal of Statistical Mechanics: Theory and Experiment*, 10, P10008.

Cafarella, M. & Cutting D. (2004). Building Nutch: Open Source Search. *ACM Queue*, 2(2), pp. 54–61.

Cortright, J. & Mayer, H. (2001). *High Tech Specialization: A Comparison of High Technology Centers*. Washington, DC: Brookings Institution, Center on Urban and Metropolitan Policy.

Eurostat (2021). Manufacturing Statistics Report, available at: https:// ec .europa .eu/ eurostat/ statistics -explained/ index .php ?title = Manufacturing _statistics _ -_NACE_Rev._2#Structural_profile accessed 15 January 2024.

Fan, J.P.H. & Lang, L.H.P. (2000). The measurement of relatedness: An application to corporate diversification. *Journal of Business*, 73(4), pp. 629–660.

Flynn, B.B., Huo, B. & Zhao, X. (2010). The impact of supply chain integration on performance: A contingency and configuration approach. *Journal of Operations Management*, 28(1), pp. 58–71.

Gök, A., Shapira, P., Klochikhin, E. & Sensier, M. (2014). Probing 'green' industry enterprises in the UK: A new identification approach. *Technological Forecasting and Social Change*, 85, pp. 93–104.

Gök, A., Waterworth, A. & Shapira, P. (2015). Use of web mining in studying innovation. *Scientometrics*, 102(1), pp. 653–671.

Grant, R.M. (1995). Toward a knowledge-based theory of the firm. *Strategic Management Journal*. Winter special issue, 17, pp. 109–122.

Heroux-Vaillancourt, M., Beaudry, C. & Rietsch, C. (2016). Validation of a web mining technique to measure innovation in the Canadian nanotechnology-related community. *Quantitative Science Studies*, 1(4), pp. 1601–1637.

Hitt, M.A., Ireland, R.D., Camp, S.M. & Sexton, D.L. (2002). Strategic entrepreneurship: Creating a new mindset, 1–16.

Kronemeyer, L., Eilers, K., Wustmans, M. & Moehrle, M. (2021). Monitoring competitors' innovation activities: Analyzing the competitive patent landscape based on semantic anchor points. *IEEE Transactions on Engineering Management*, 68(5), pp. 1272–1287.

Lancichinetti, A. & Fortunato, S. (2009). Community detection algorithms: A comparative analysis. *Physical Review E*, 80(5), 056117.

Libaers, D., Hicks, D. & Porter, A.L. (2010). A taxonomy of small firm technology commercialization. *Industrial and Corporate Change*, 25(3), pp. 371–405.

Marra, A., Antonelli, P., Dell'Anna, L., & Pozzi, C. (2015). A network analysis using metadata to investigate innovation in clean-tech – Implications for energy policy. *Energy Policy*, 86, pp. 17–26.

Marra, A., Baldassari, C. & Carlei, V. (2020). Exploring networks of proximity for partner selection, firms' collaboration and knowledge exchange. The case of clean-tech industry. *Business Strategy and the Environment*, 29, pp. 1034–1044.

Marra, A., Cassetta, E. & Antonelli, P. (2017). Emerging specialisations and software metropolitan clusters – a comparative network analysis on San Francisco, New York and London. *International Journal of Technological Learning, Innovation and Development*, 9(1), pp. 17–41.

Matyjas, Z. (2014). The role of the structure-conduct-performance paradigm for the development of industrial organization economics and strategic management. *Journal of Positive Management*, 5(2), pp. 53–63.

Milara, M. (2014). Comparison of resources and capabilities in two companies. Universitat jaume. Retrieved from http://repositori.uji.es/xmlui/bitstream/handle/10234/97662/TFG_2014_MALOI.PDF?sequence=4 accessed 15 January 2024.

Mills, J., Platts, K., Bourne, M. & Richards, H. (2002). *Strategy and Performance: Competing Through Competences*. Cambridge: Cambridge University Press.

Nathan, M. & Rosso, A. (2015). Mapping digital businesses with big data: Some early findings from the UK. *Research Policy*, 44(9), pp. 1714–1733.

Papagiannidis, S., See-To, E.W.H., Assimakopoulos, D.G. & Yang, Y. (2018). Identifying industrial clusters with a novel big-data methodology: Are SIC codes (not) fit for purpose in the Internet age? *Computers and Operations*, 98, pp. 355–366.

Peteraf, M.A. (1993). The cornerstones of competitive advantage: A resource-based view. *Strategic Management Journal*, 14(3), pp. 179–191.

Pons, P. & Latapy, M. (2006). Computing communities in large networks using random walks. *Journal of Graph Algorithms and Applications*, 10(2), pp. 191–218.

Powell, T.C. (2001). Competitive advantage: Logical and philosophical considerations. *Strategic Management Journal*, 22, pp. 875–888.

Shapira, P., Youtie, J. & Kay L. (2011). National innovation system dynamics in the globalization of nano-technology innovation. *The Journal of Technology Transfer*, 36(6), pp. 587–604.

Staccioli, J. & Virgillito, M.E. (2021). The present, past, and future of labor-saving technologies. In K.F., Zimmermann (ed.), *Handbook of Labor, Human Resources and Population Economics*. Springer, cham. (pp. 1–16).

Stathoulopoulos, K. & Mateos-Garcia, J. (2017). Mapping without a map: Exploring the UK business landscape using unsupervised learning. SocArXiv ryxdk, Center for Open Science.

8. Identifying business models through the analysis of corporate websites

Marco Chiaromonte and Marco Cucculelli

1.   INTRODUCTION

In recent years, the analysis of business models has gained considerable importance in economics. Understanding the business models used by companies is indeed crucial for evaluating their economic and financial performance and identifying strategies for success in specific industries.

The main purpose of this chapter is to investigate the business models of established companies through an in-depth analysis of their corporate websites. Specifically, it aims to investigate the feasibility of defining companies' business models using website analysis, to determine whether there is a specific business model that is prevalent in the industry, and to investigate the relationship between the adopted business model and companies' economic and financial performance. In this respect, we hypothesize that companies that choose a business model similar to the one prevailing in the industry tend to achieve average returns, while companies adopting a business model that differs from the average business model of that industry can achieve different results.

Importantly, we retrieve corporate business models by analysing the companies' websites. In today's digital age, the Internet has become a critical tool for companies to reach their customer segments, both in the B2C and B2B markets. A well-presented corporate image and a clear articulation of business activities are essential to attract customers and achieve business goals. Websites have gained even more importance in the wake of the COVID-19 pandemic: distinctive website design and customer satisfaction play a crucial role in the B2C market, while the company's vision is becoming increasingly important in the B2B market; a concise but compelling presentation of the company's structure along the entire value chain is also essential. Various studies have shown a positive correlation between perceived service quality on websites and consumer purchase intent. Companies that do not adhere to website parameters and do not fully exploit the potential of their website may thus struggle to be successful (Yoo and Donthu 2001; Loiacono et al. 2002; Ranganathan and Ganapathy 2002).

The balance of this chapter is organized as follows: Section 2 describes the sample design and the methodology used for data collection and analysis; Section 3 presents the main results of the empirical analysis by illustrating the prevalent business models, the performance indicators of the companies, and the main characteristics of the companies grouped in different clusters. Section 4 concludes.

2.   DATA AND METHODOLOGY

2.1   Sample Characteristics and Sample Selection

For the present analysis, we selected a sample of Italian SMEs (which are part of the companies that took part in the survey described in the Appendix of this book) based on the sector they operate (the manufacturing sector and manufacturing-related services) and the availability of corporate websites. To ensure homogeneity, the first and last percentiles were excluded (5 per cent), and a sales-based upper limit was set. Since several companies were sold, merged or went bankrupt during the analysis period, or websites were simply no longer available, the final sample comprises 1,946 companies.

2.2   A Compact Overview of the Methodology

The analysis unfolded through the following three main phases:

Phase I: Analysis of the websites
Each website was analysed by three different coders.

To mitigate the discretionary and subjective effect of direct inspection, each company was indeed assigned to three different coders for analysis. The coders are a group of post-doctoral students from Università Politecnica delle Marche who possess an in-depth background in economics and business, and who received proper training before starting the assigned task. At this stage, companies were randomly assigned to coders and not aggregated by sector to prevent the analysis from being influenced by the business model prevalent in the sector.

Coders were provided with two different modules that were uploaded to the Google Forms platform. The first module was intended for the analysis of the individual websites, while the second module was used for the distribution of the companies among the different categories. A table was created containing the nine building blocks theorized by Osterwalder and Pigneur (2010; see Figures 8A.1a and b in the appendix to this chapter), as well as their main components. Specifically, the form consisted of a total of 29 questions divided into two parts: the first one covered all the possible elements of a business model and focused on identifying the business model chosen by a company. The second part aimed to analyse other overarching aspects of business models that have gained importance in recent years, such as the development of circular economy activities, processes or environmentally friendly products and activities, and data analysis, which significantly support business performance and signal a company's responsiveness to market pressures.

Phase II: Identification of the companies' business models
In this phase, each analyst identified the company's business model based on the data collected by their peers and determined the business model of each company based on the previous rounds of interpretation of the websites. If different answers emerged for the same 'building block', the analyst conducted a further round of analysis to integrate the spectrum of data collected and determine the correct structural element.

Phase III: Identification of the prevailing business model in each sector and classification of the companies into different categories
Once the business models of all the sampled companies were identified, they were classified into segments based on the three-digit ATECO 2007 codes. In this way, analysts retrieved the predominant business model in each sector and defined the 'sectoral' business model. As expected, it was almost always possible to recover the prevailing business model, with only a few companies deviating from the sector average business model. In addition, analysts were asked to examine companies that introduced business models that deviated from the industry average or were characterized by disruptive or innovative features. At this stage, analysts were provided with a complete dataset of economic and financial indices, financial ratios, and other functional elements for industry and company analysis. Specifically, for each company, analysts were given information on the year of establishment, the 2016–2018 revenue growth rate, the 2016–2018 average ROS and the number of employees, so that they could link firm performance to the business model. Additionally, coders were provided with sectoral financial data for the period 2018–2019, that is, median ROS, median number of employees, median revenues and median growth rate, which they used to make comparisons between individual performance and average industry performance.

After that, the analysts were asked to determine the industry average business model using a form made up of six sections (Figure 8A.2 in the appendix to this chapter): the first section, which concerns the industry average, aimed to detect the prevailing BM within the industry; the second section focused on the identification of the best-performing company in the industry based on economic and financial metrics, with particular emphasis on the company's growth rate; the third section aimed at identifying the worst-performing companies in the industry; the fourth section was devoted to analysing potentially 'disruptive' companies; the fifth section was intended to host potentially 'innovative' companies. Finally, the last section collected 'residual' companies, that is, companies that pursue a business model that deviates from the industry average but cannot be classified in any of the aforementioned categories. More information on each category is reported in Section 2.3.

2.3   Data Collection and Firm Classification

In this section, we provide a more detailed account of the selected methodology. As anticipated above, the first phase intended to identify the business model of the sampled companies, starting from the analysis of the corporate websites. The analysts were asked to access the website in advance and conduct a detailed investigation aimed at gathering the information required for the identification of the BM. Then, the analysts filled in the forms on the Google Forms platform to collect the results.

BOX 8.1   ALPHA COMPANY

This example is intended to illustrate how the information on the company 'Alpha''s website was collected to describe the adopted BM.

The 'Products' page states that the company 'uses a global network of national and international suppliers to select the most suitable partner in terms of technology and production capacity for each product. The company adopts an open, multidisciplinary approach that allows it to deal with the most advanced logistics and production practises that the market offers.' It highlights the strategic importance of partnerships and suppliers, and it is possible to characterize two structural segments of the company BM.

Further analysis of the 'Products' page shows that Alpha's value proposition is clearly focused on service and not exclusively on the sale of physical goods.

The 'Solutions' page presents the different types of products and services offered and allows description of the company's 'value proposition' based on product performance, problem-solving approach (key activity) and customer customization.

Alpha appears on the 'Stakeholders' page as a B2B company focused on partnerships and co-engineering. It is possible to identify the markets reached, B2B (channels) and the importance of partnerships (key partnerships) and co-engineering processes (customer relationship).

On the 'Competences' page, it says: 'The internal experience of our team allows us to be a strong and efficient partner in the following areas: electronics (hardware, software/firmware), mechanics, industrial design, laboratory testing (safety, EMC, climatic testing), certification and industrial production. These characteristics have allowed us to achieve the highest standards of innovation, quality, production flexibility and economic efficiency.'

It can be seen that the company is diversifying market segmentation, as customer segments have different problems. It can also be seen that human resources are of great importance to the company (key resources).

From the analysis of the implicit information on the website, all the other characteristics of the business model can be inferred, such as the revenue model and the distribution channels used by the company.

In the second phase, analysts used the results of the website analysis of phase 1 to identify the business model of each company. If a building block could not be defined (less than two out of three collected data matched), the analyst had to perform a new analysis to identify the most accurate structural element. Analysts were also asked to retrieve implicit information that could lead to a particular 'building block' when the BM structural elements did not clearly emerge from the website analysis. Once the BMs were identified, the companies included in the sample were classified into homogeneous sectors (defined at the ATECO 2007 – 3-digit level).

The final phase began with the identification of the business model prevalent in the sectors, its characteristics and peculiarities. The companies were grouped into the following categories:

- Companies whose business model is in line with the industry's one: this category includes companies that share at least seven (out of nine) characteristics with the business model that prevails in the industry.
- Best Performers: companies in this group exhibit significantly above-average overall performance. The main parameter used to determine this group was the company's growth rate; secondary parameters such as ROS, sales, and number of employees were also taken into account.
- Worst Performers: as in the case of the best performers, the companies in this group were identified based on their business performance. These companies display below-average performance based on factors such as growth rate, ROS, sales, and number of employees.
- Innovative Companies: this category includes companies whose business model presents elements of novelty or innovation compared to other com-

panies. Only companies that were recognized as 'innovative' by all the coders were included in this group.

- Disruptive Companies: these firms exhibit elements of disruption or uniqueness in their business models compared to other companies. Again, only companies that were labelled 'disruptive' by all the coders were placed in this category.
- Residual Companies: this group includes all the companies that do not fall into any of the previous categories, namely, companies whose business model differs from the average, are not considered unique or innovative, and/or have an average performance within the sector.

3.   MAIN RESULTS OF THE EMPIRICAL ANALYSIS

From the implementation of the empirical analysis, it emerges that our initial hypothesis was correct, namely, that companies with similar business models often have comparable economic and financial performance. This correlation can be attributed to several factors; first, companies operating with the same business model tend to face similar market conditions, customer preferences, and competitive dynamics, which may contribute to comparable financial performance. In addition, the adoption of similar business models often implies the use of comparable strategies, operational processes, and approaches to revenue generation, which can lead to parallel performance patterns.

Concerning the identification of a prevalent business model in the industry, the empirical results show that the majority of companies in each sector follow a prevailing and well-defined 'sectoral' model.

The third important result concerns the relationship between the adoption of a particular business model and firm performance: in most cases, companies that use a business model that differs from the industry average business model exhibit a performance that deviates from the industry average one. The few companies whose business model diverges from the average one are those that use disruptive or innovative business models or different building blocks. A more detailed description of the main results of our study is provided in Section 3.1.

3.1   Sectoral Analysis

As mentioned earlier, it was possible to identify the average (i.e., prevailing) business model of 38 different industry segments categorised according to the 3-digit ATECO 2007 code, as shown in Table 8.1.

We can see that almost all industries appear to serve segmented markets and use direct sales channels, such as internal sales and e-commerce; customer relationships are based primarily on customer service, with a preference for

Table 8.1   *The analysed sectors. ATECO 2007 – 3-digit categorization*

ATECO	Description	ATECO	Description
141	Clothing and leather manufacturing	310	Furniture manufacturing
152	Footwear manufacturing	331	Metal items and machinery maintenance
162	Wood items manufacturing	332	Industrial machinery installation
172	Paper items manufacturing	432	Electrical and hydraulic plant installation
181	Printing and printing services	451	Motorized vehicle trading
221	Rubber items manufacturing	452	Motorized vehicle maintenance
222	Plastic items manufacturing	464	Final consumer goods wholesale
251	Metal items manufacturing	465	ICT device wholesale
255	Metal forging and printing	466	Other machinery and facilities wholesale
256	Metal coating	467	Specialized wholesale
257	Knife and hardware manufacturing	522	Supporting transport business
259	Other metal items manufacturing	619	Other telecommunication business
261	Electronic hardware manufacturing	620	Software development and IT consulting
265	Measurement tool manufacturing	631	Data processing
271	Engine, electric transformer manuf.	712	Acceptance test plan
279	Other electric manufacturing	721	R&D in engineering
282	Other machinery manufacturing	731	Advertisement
284	Metal shaping machinery manuf.	741	Design
289	Other special machinery manuf.	749	Other professional and scientific business

personal support. The value proposition of the surveyed companies focuses primarily on achieving high-performance standards for their products/services, problem-solving approaches, and co-designing products and services with customer involvement. The revenue model is essentially based on direct payment for an asset, with pricing at a premium. The cost structure appears to be focused on value creation rather than cost minimization. The main resources are fixed assets and human capital. In addition, the most important activities are production and problem-solving aimed at finding the best solutions for the customer. Also, strategic alliances with non-competitors are proving to be critical key partnerships.

From the association between the business model retrieved by the coders and the financial data, it emerges that the majority of the companies adopting the average business model achieve an economic-financial performance that is in line with the average one of the segment. If we compare the median sector parameters (sales, growth, ROS) with those of the company, we see that only 13 per cent of them differ in sales (+/- 75 per cent compared to the sector average) and growth rate (+/- 150 per cent compared to the sector average) in all 38 segments of the sample, while 8 per cent of the firms show significant differences in the ROS (+/-50 per cent compared to the industry average). In summary, more than 90 per cent of the companies adopting the industry average BM are performing in line with the industry average.

3.2   Identification of the Best Performers

To identify the best-performing companies in the sector, four financial indices (i.e., average ROS, average growth rate, average revenue and average number of employees) at the sectoral level were computed and then compared with the firm-level indicators.

To illustrate the business model divergence between the best-performing and average companies in the sector, we used the Business Model Contrast Index (hereafter BMCI). The index was calculated as the quotient of the number of building blocks that differ from the industry average and the number of total building blocks: for example, a BMCI of 33 per cent means that a company has a business model that differs from the industry average in three out of nine of the building blocks that make up a business model.

Across the 38 sectors analysed, 78 companies, which present an average BMCI of 32.46 per cent, were identified as best performers. Compared to the average sector results, in the best performers revenues are higher by 446 per cent, the growth rate is higher by 275 per cent, the ROS is higher by 207 per cent, and the number of employees is higher by 268 per cent. These findings could be attributable to these companies' ability to identify the average business model weaknesses and activate business model reconfiguration processes.

3.3   Identification of the Worst Performers

The worst-performing companies in the industry were identified using the same procedure adopted for the best-performing companies.

The worst-performing companies display a BMCI equal to 31.4 per cent. On average, a deviation from the average business model of the sector leads to a performance that differs (is either better or worse) from the average performance of the segment. Seventy-eight companies with the worst performance were identified in the various sectors of the sample.

When the median of the indices is calculated, we see that, in the worst-performing companies, revenues are 80 per cent lower than the average one, the growth rate is 320 per cent lower, the ROS is 257 per cent lower, and the number of employees is 60 per cent lower.

All in all, it seems that deviating from the industry average BM may not only improve business performance, but also imply risks that negatively impact business results.

3.4 Identification of Firms with 'Disruptive' or 'Innovative' Business Models

Categories 4 and 5 comprise firms whose business models present disruptive or innovative characteristics. Disruptive business models are business models presenting distinctive features that cannot be found in any other company in the sector. Innovative business models are, instead, business models that exhibit characteristics of novelty and innovation that are rarely found in other companies in the industry. To provide a more objective analysis, the study only considered business models that were unanimously (i.e., by the three coders and the project managers) classified as disruptive or innovative.

These disruptive and innovative business models were found in 2.3 per cent and 3.9 per cent of the companies studied, respectively: across the different sectors of the sample, 42 companies were classified as 'unique', while 72 companies were labelled 'innovative'. Interestingly, the data analysis reveals that 56.8 per cent of the companies applying disruptive business models outperform. The disruptive business models have a BMCI of 43 per cent, experience high growth rates (+104 per cent) and ROS (+38 per cent) despite slightly underperforming revenues (-10 per cent) and a below-average (-12 per cent) firm size.

Concerning innovative business models, 62.5 per cent of them display an above-average performance and present a BMCI equal to 56 per cent. These companies report lower revenues than the industry average (-48 per cent), but also high growth rates and ROS (+223 per cent and +130 per cent, respectively). The size of the company appears to be smaller, as the percentage of employees is lower than the industry average by 54 per cent. A compact account of innovative and disruptive business models is offered in Figure 8.1.

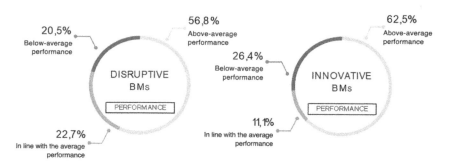

Figure 8.1   *Disruptive and innovative BMs percentage categorization by performance*

3.5   'Residual' Firms

The companies that did not fall into any of the previously discussed categories were classified as 'residual'. They amount to 193, and correspond to about 10 per cent of the sample; this means that, on average, only ten out of 100 companies in the sector adopted a business model that deviates from the prevailing model but, at the same time, have a performance in line with the industry average one.

4.   CONCLUSION

This chapter presents an original empirical analysis which identifies business models through the analysis of the companies' websites. We show that more than 90 per cent of companies operating in homogeneous segments tend to use similar business models: by aligning themselves with the average industry business model, companies are able to achieve performance levels that are in line with the industry average in terms of revenue, growth rate, and ROS. In a similar vein, companies that deviate from the industry average business model had performance results that differ from the industry average. This suggests that adopting a business model that diverges from the 'standard' exposes companies to both the risk of achieving performance results that are either higher or lower than average.

These results thus point to a relationship between firm performance and the chosen business model. In this context, company size, proxied by the number of employees, matters as well: in most cases, the companies with divergent business models are smaller than companies in the same segment. Smaller firms can more easily adapt and experiment with different business models because of their flexibility, while larger companies may face challenges in implementing change because of their organizational complexity and rigidity, and because they can find it hard to communicate business model changes to a larger workforce.

Accordingly, the study sheds light on the complex relationship between business models, performance outcomes and organizational characteristics, and provides valuable insights for companies seeking to optimize their strategies and achieve sustained success in their respective industries. Future research could explore further nuances of business model adoption and adaptation in response to dynamic market conditions and emerging industrial trends.

REFERENCES

Loiacono, E.T., Watson, R.T. & Goodhue, D.L. (2002) WebQual: A measure of website quality. *Marketing Theory and Applications*, 13, 432–438.

Osterwalder, A. & Pigneur, Y. (2010). *Business Model Generation: A Handbook for Visionaries, Game Changers, and Challengers*. John Wiley & Sons.

Ranganathan, C. & Ganapathy, S. (2002) Key dimensions of business-to-consumer web sites. *Information and Management*, 39(6), 457–465. doi:10.1016/S0378-7206(01)00112-4.

Yoo, B. & Donthu, N. (2001) Developing and validating a multidimensional consumer-based brand equity scale. *Journal of Business Research*, 52, 1–14.

APPENDIX

1. COMPANY'S NAME *

_____

2. VAT NUMBER *

_____

3. WEBSITE YEAR PUBLISHING

_____

4. WEBSITES NUMBER OF PAGES

_____

5. 1 – CUSTOMER SEGMENTS *

Contrassegna solo un ovale.

○ Mass market
○ Niche market
○ Segmented Market
○ Diversified Market
○ Multisided Market
○ N/A

6. 2 – CHANNELS *

Seleziona tutte le voci applicabili.

☐ Direct owner channels
☐ Indirect owner channels
☐ Indirect partner channels
☐ N/A

7. The firm operate in a market: *

Seleziona tutte le voci applicabili.

☐ B2B
☐ B2C

8. 3 – CUSTOMER RELATIONSHIP *

Seleziona tutte le voci applicabili.

☐ Personal assistance
☐ Dedicated personal assistance
☐ Self-service
☐ Web Community
☐ Co-creation
☐ N/A

9. 4 – VALUE PROPOSITION *

Seleziona tutte le voci applicabili.

☐ Novelty
☐ Performance
☐ Customisation
☐ Problem Solving
☐ Design
☐ Brand/status symbol
☐ Price
☐ Productive efficiency
☐ Risk reduction
☐ Accessibility
☐ N/A

10. The company's value proposition focuses on: *

Seleziona tutte le voci applicabili.

☐ Products
☐ Services
☐ Servitisation
☐ Range of proucts
☐ N/A

11. 5 – REVENUE MODEL *

Seleziona tutte le voci applicabili.

☐ Direct payment of an asset/markup
☐ Usage/pay-per-use fee
☐ Subscription fees
☐ Loan/rental/leasing
☐ Licenses
☐ Brokerage fees
☐ Advertisements
☐ Interest
☐ N/A

12. The firm's price list is: *

Seleziona tutte le voci applicabili.

☐ Fixed price list
☐ Dynamic price list
☐ N/A

13. 6 – Key Resources *

Contrassegna solo un ovale.

○ Physical Resources
○ Financial resources
○ Intellectual Resources
○ Human Resources
○ N/A

14. 7 – KEY ACTIVITIES *

Contrassegna solo un ovale.

○ Production
○ Problem solving
○ Platform/network
○ N/A

15. 8 – KEY PARTNERSHIP *

Seleziona tutte le voci applicabili.

☐ Strategic alliances between competitors
☐ Strategic alliances between non-competitors
☐ Joint Venture
☐ Buyer–supplier relationships
☐ University relationships
☐ None of the above
☐ N/A

Figure 8A.1a　Business model identification form – Part 1

16. **The partnership purpose is:** *

Contrassegna solo un ovale.

- ○ Economies of scale
- ○ Risk reduction
- ○ Resource and skill acquisition
- ○ Product/service improvement
- ○ N/A

17. **9 – COST STRUCTURE** *

Contrassegna solo un ovale.

- ○ Cost reduction
- ○ Creation of premium value
- ○ N/A

18. **COST STRUCTURE IS BASED ON:**

Seleziona tutte le voci applicabili.

- ☐ Fixed costs
- ☐ Variable costs
- ☐ Economies of scales
- ☐ Economies of scope
- ☐ N/A

19. **Indicate the three most relevant building blocks:**

Seleziona tutte le voci applicabili.

	1	2	3	4	5
1) CUSTOMER SEGMENTS	☐	☐	☐	☐	☐
2) CHANNELS	☐	☐	☐	☐	☐
3) CUSTOMER RELATIONSHIP	☐	☐	☐	☐	☐
4) VALUE PROPOSITION	☐	☐	☐	☐	☐
5) REVENUE MODEL	☐	☐	☐	☐	☐
6) KEY RESOURCES	☐	☐	☐	☐	☐
7) KEY ACTIVITIES	☐	☐	☐	☐	☐
8) KEY PARTNERSHIPS	☐	☐	☐	☐	☐
9) COST STRUCTURE	☐	☐	☐	☐	☐

20. **The analysed BM could be considered "disruptive"?** *

Contrassegna solo un ovale.

- ○ Yes
- ○ No

21. **The analysed BM could be considered "innovative"?** *

Contrassegna solo un ovale.

- ○ Yes
- ○ No

22. **Based on the website analysis, the firm has:** *

Seleziona tutte le voci applicabili.

- ☐ Vertically integrated activities or processes
- ☐ Horizontally integrated activities or processes
- ☐ Financially integrated other businesses
- ☐ N/A

23. **Has the company implemented Green Economy projects?** *

Contrassegna solo un ovale.

- ○ Yes
- ○ No
- ○ N/A

24. **Has the company implemented Circular Economy projects?** *

Contrassegna solo un ovale.

- ○ Yes
- ○ No
- ○ N/A

25. **Is the company active on data analysis processes (Data analytics, Big data, etc.)?** *

Contrassegna solo un ovale.

- ○ Yes
- ○ No
- ○ N/A

26. **Is the firm exploiting data to achieve a competitive advantage?** *

Contrassegna solo un ovale.

- ○ Yes
- ○ No
- ○ N/A

27. **Suggest further matters not emerging from the survey:**

_____
_____
_____
_____
_____

28. **Suggest five key-words able to define the company's BM:** *

_____

Figure 8A.1b   Business model identification form – Part 2

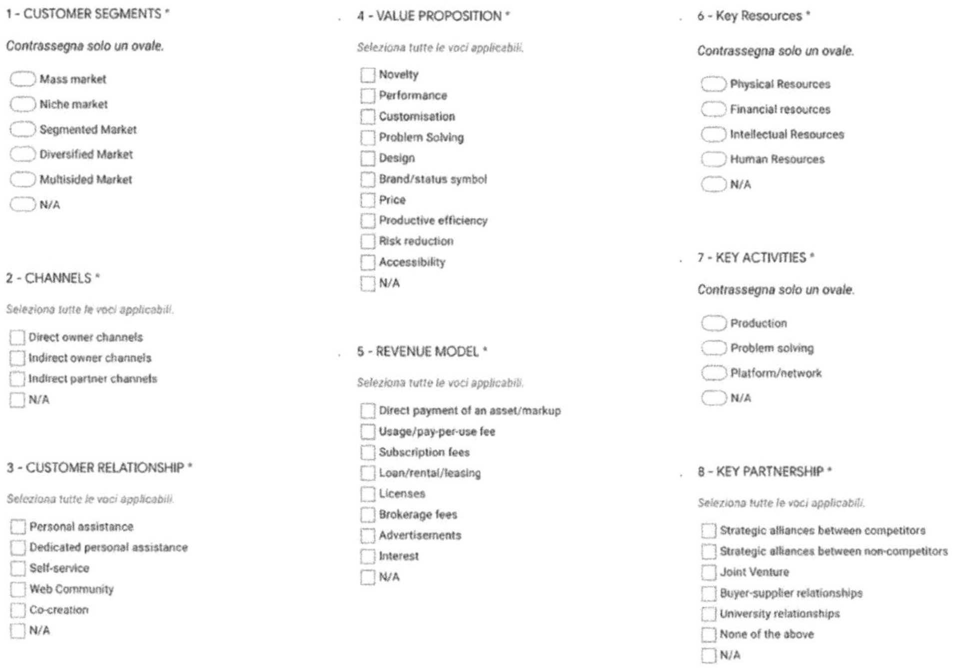

9 - COST STRUCTURE *

Contrassegna solo un ovale.

○ Cost reduction
○ Creation of premium value
○ N/A

6 - Key Resources *

Contrassegna solo un ovale.

○ Physical Resources
○ Financial resources
○ Intellectual Resources
○ Human Resources
○ N/A

7 - KEY ACTIVITIES *

Contrassegna solo un ovale.

○ Production
○ Problem solving
○ Platform/network
○ N/A

8 - KEY PARTNERSHIP *

Seleziona tutte le voci applicabili.

☐ Strategic alliances between competitors
☐ Strategic alliances between non-competitors
☐ Joint Venture
☐ Buyer-supplier relationships
☐ University relationships
☐ None of the above
☐ N/A

4 - VALUE PROPOSITION *

Seleziona tutte le voci applicabili.

☐ Novelty
☐ Performance
☐ Customisation
☐ Problem Solving
☐ Design
☐ Brand/status symbol
☐ Price
☐ Productive efficiency
☐ Risk reduction
☐ Accessibility
☐ N/A

5 - REVENUE MODEL *

Seleziona tutte le voci applicabili.

☐ Direct payment of an asset/markup
☐ Usage/pay-per-use fee
☐ Subscription fees
☐ Loan/rental/leasing
☐ Licenses
☐ Brokerage fees
☐ Advertisements
☐ Interest
☐ N/A

1 - CUSTOMER SEGMENTS *

Contrassegna solo un ovale.

○ Mass market
○ Niche market
○ Segmented Market
○ Diversified Market
○ Multisided Market
○ N/A

2 - CHANNELS *

Seleziona tutte le voci applicabili.

☐ Direct owner channels
☐ Indirect owner channels
☐ Indirect partner channels
☐ N/A

3 - CUSTOMER RELATIONSHIP *

Seleziona tutte le voci applicabili.

☐ Personal assistance
☐ Dedicated personal assistance
☐ Self-service
☐ Web Community
☐ Co-creation
☐ N/A

Figure 8A.2   Classification of firms and prevailing BM identification form

Appendix: the survey

Marco Chiaromonte and Marco Cucculelli

1. INTRODUCTION

The rapid progress of digital technologies has significantly transformed industries worldwide. In the context of Industry 4.0, these advancements hold the potential to transform manufacturing processes, increase productivity, and drive economic growth. Understanding the adoption and planning rates of Industry 4.0 technologies and their connections with the restructuring of business models is critical for policymakers, industry leaders, and researchers to effectively leverage these innovations.

To this purpose, we designed a survey aimed at gaining detailed information on various business aspects, including the firms' position in the value chain, their green innovation activities, their data use practices, their investment policies, in addition to their business model transformation strategies and their approaches to technology adoption. By targeting specific areas of inquiry, the survey was intended to provide a comprehensive understanding of companies' practices and the challenges associated with integrating new technologies into new business models.

2. AN OVERVIEW OF THE SURVEY

Most studies of corporate behaviour focus on large, publicly traded companies listed on the official market. Large amounts of data are usually available for these companies. Useful information to assess the stock market's response to major changes in the company's business behaviour and to understand how companies compete in the market can be obtained from various sources such as company balance sheets, stock market transactions, company annual reports, and the specialized press. However, this type of information is not available for the majority of companies operating in the small business sector: in this case, apart from company balance sheets, publicly available data sources usually do not contain information on the main factors affecting business behaviour, and most data can only be obtained through direct interviews. In light of thes-considerations, we created a dataset by matching two complementary sources: (i) a cross-sectional dataset based on first-hand information collected directly from firms through questionnaire-based interviews and (ii) a dataset from Bureau van Dijk consisting of company financial statements.

In this section, we briefly present our survey; in particular, we provide some information on sample selection and data collection, sample representativeness, and baseline statistics, and report the questions used to build the variables on business model innovation variables that were used in the regression analysis of some chapters of this book.

2.1   Sample Selection

In early 2019, we developed a survey with the aim of shedding light on relevant business aspects of Italian manufacturing companies that are often difficult to identify and describe. To this end, between May and June 2019, we conducted a pilot test to evaluate the functionality of the online platform to which we intended to upload the questionnaire. Then, using the AIDA-Bvd database, we identified all Italian companies operating in the manufacturing and manufacturing-related sectors according to the ATECO/NACE Rev.2 classification (i.e., companies whose two-digit ATECO/NACE is between 10 and 33, and ATECO/NACE 62, 63 and 71) and whose number of employees in 2019 was smaller than 1,000. In doing so, we excluded very large firms, which could exhibit peculiar dynamics, and obtained a quite representative picture of the universe of Italian firms. The number of companies that matched these criteria was about 600,000; to attain a handleable initial sample, we randomly selected about 10 per cent of the firms contained in the Aida list, which amounted to around 60,000. This initial sample seems to be sufficiently representative of the Italian economic structure, as it is consistent with the distribution of the North-western and Central regions of the country, while there is a slight deviation between the Northeast and the South of Italy (Table A.1).

Table A.1   *Firms distribution by area: comparison between sample and population*

Sample break down	%	Firm population	%
North-west	31%	North-west	29%
North-east	31%	North-east	21%
Central	23%	Central	22%
South	15%	South	20%

Source: Authors' elaboration of survey data.

It must be acknowledged, however, that some limitations exist. For example, the sample may not include all possible manufacturing and manufacturing-related firms in Italy, and certain industries or regions may be underrepresented despite the stratification process. In addition, the survey procedure may be subject to inherent biases, such as non-response or self-selection, which are frequent in this type of empirical investigation.

2.2   Data Collection

The data collection was conducted between October 2019 and February 2020. This time frame allowed for extended data collection that ensured comprehensive coverage and gave the respondents adequate time to complete the questionnaire. Survey methods and the specific time frame were carefully selected to maximize participation rates and provide a robust data set for analysis. In order to obtain more accurate and reliable responses and increase the chances of participation, we involved a team of graduate students with professional experience in the fields of economics and business who, under our supervision, contacted the entrepreneurs and managers of the selected companies and assisted them in responding.

The companies were reached either by phone or by e-mail. Using the first method, which we applied to the selected companies that had at least 50 employees in 2019 (i.e., approximately 11,700 companies), the analysts managed to establish a direct, effective, and tailored communication in which they could provide useful information and eliminate possible doubts. Throughout the data collection process, analysts carefully monitored the questionnaires' completion status and response rate, sending reminders to companies whose questionnaires were still incomplete. To maintain a consistent response rate, the analysts contacted the companies if the questionnaire was still incomplete after a reasonable period of time. This follow-up served as a gentle reminder and encouragement for respondents to complete the questionnaire. By proactively addressing potential obstacles, analysts sought to maximize response rates and ensure a representative sample. As a gesture of appreciation for the companies' participation and cooperation, the analysts sent thank-you e-mails to all companies engaged in the survey.

In the second approach, an e-mail was sent to small businesses, that is, those with fewer than 50 employees in 2019, with information about the questionnaire and the link to the online platform. To achieve a higher response rate, reminder e-mails were sent to the companies that had not completed the questionnaire within the established deadlines. The purpose of these reminder e-mails was to encourage and prompt respondents to complete the questionnaire in order to increase the overall participation rate. This method proved to be particularly beneficial in reaching a larger number of companies within the sample, thus increasing the overall coverage and representativeness of the study.

At the end of the data collection, we obtained 16,492 questionnaires (out of the original sample of 55,124 companies); thus, the response rate was approximately 29.9 per cent. We then reviewed the responses and discarded questionnaires that were significantly incomplete (n. = 2,705) or contained potentially unreliable information, as well as duplicates and companies that had exited the market in the meantime (n. =5,278); in this way, we ended up with 8,509 usable questionnaires.

We have checked the representativeness of both the total sample of respondents (consisting of 8,509 firms) and subsamples of firms used in the empirical analysis presented in some of the book chapters by comparing the distribution of firms in both samples with (i) the distribution observed in our original dataset (i.e., the 55,124 firms mentioned above) and (ii) the firm distribution based on national data on Italian manufacturing firms compiled by the Italian Statistical Institute (ISTAT). As can be seen from Figure A.1, the distribution of firms among Italian NUTS-2 regions does not significantly vary across the datasets. This is also true for the final sample used for the empirical analyses, with the exception of a slight overrepresentation of the Veneto and Marche regions and, to a lesser extent, Emilia Romagna.

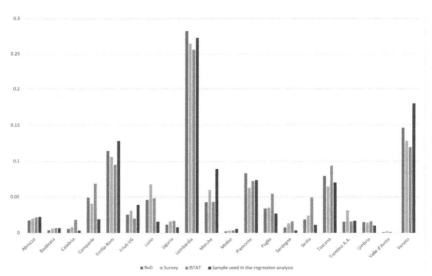

Source: Authors' elaboration of data from the survey, Aida BvD and ISTAT.

Figure A.1   *Distribution of firms by NUTS-2 regions (regional share) across different datasets*

Overall, the responses of the sampled companies show a remarkable concentration in the northern regions of Italy, as about 62 per cent of the completed questionnaires come from this area (Figure A.2). This high response rate reflects the active participation and commitment of companies in the northern part of the country. Participation in the central regions was also notable, with around 23 per cent of the total responses. In contrast, the response rate in the southern region was relatively low, representing about 15 per cent of the completed questionnaires.

SAMPLE DISTRIBUTION BY REGION

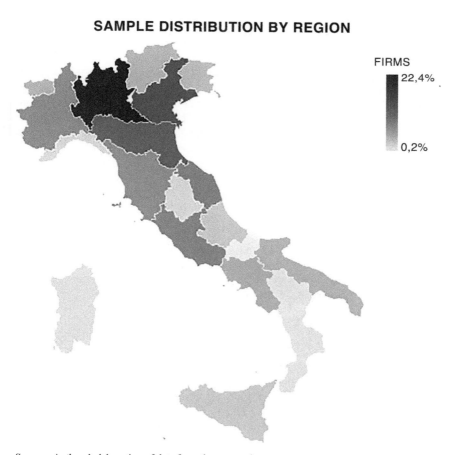

Source: Authors' elaboration of data from the survey data.

Figure A.2   Sample distribution by regions

2.3   The Structure of the Survey

The survey questionnaire comprises the following six distinct sections, each addressing specific aspects of the companies' operations and strategies:

(1)   Company's General Information: it aims to provide an overview of the companies' financial performance and market dynamics by collecting information on variables such as firm turnover, export activities, and the impact of key customers on revenue generation.

(2)   Business Model Innovation: this section focuses on the changes made by companies to their business model in the previous years in four relevant functional areas.

(3)   Adopted or Planned Industry 4.0 Technologies: this part of the questionnaire explores the effective or planned development and implementation of new digital and enabling technologies, such as Big Data, Cloud Computing, Cyber Security, Additive Manufacturing and Collaborative Robots.

(4)   Data Management: the fourth section aims to shed light on the importance of data analysis for the surveyed companies; to this end, it investigates the companies' approaches to data management and their utilization of data-driven decision-making processes.

(5)   Eco-Innovation: this part explores the companies' alignment with environmentally friendly and 'green' policies and practices.

(6)   Investment Policy: the sixth section aims to advance our understanding of the companies' willingness to invest in innovative technologies, processes, or market expansion.

Finally, the survey included a final section gathering information (e.g., age, gender, role within the company) about the interviewee.

Below are reported the specific questions on business model innovation that we used in some chapters of this book:

2.1. Products and production processes
Since the last three years, the firm (report significant changes only):

- It has introduced new products
- It has added ancillary or complementary services to its main products
- It has specialized on a main product, extending its selling to markets/clients not previously served
- It has modified its client portfolio and the markets it serves
- It has introduced new and/or more efficient production processes
- It has reduced the 'Time to Market' (i.e., the length of time from the conception of a product until it is released to the market)
- None of the previous answers

2.2. Finance

Since the last three years, the firm (report significant changes only):

- It has modified its pricing policies (e.g., prices that vary with product demand, discount policies)
- It has modified its sales methods (e.g., pay-per use, rental, license or other methods)
- It has increased its revenues thanks to the introduction of ancillary or complementary services
- It has focused on mass markets
- It has focused on niche markets
- It sets fixed prices
- It sets dynamic prices (e.g., based on negotiation, based on the available supply, auction)
- None of the previous answers

2.3. Business relationships and business networks

Since the last three years, the firm: (report significant changes only)

- It has internalized upstream activities that were previously carried out by other actors of the supply chain (suppliers of raw materials, semifinished products and equipment)
- It has internalized downstream activities that were previously carried out by other actors of the supply chain (services, sales network or clients)
- It has internalized ancillary activities that support the main business
- It has outsourced activities that were previously carried out within the company
- It has modified or introduced new direct sales channels (e.g., online, e-commerce or digital, new sales networks)
- It has modified or introduced new indirect sales channels (e.g., wholesalers, distributors or other intermediaries)
- It has formalized new partnerships with clients, suppliers or competitors
- It has benefited from incentives and/or tax relief for investments (e.g., Industry 4.0)
- None of the previous answers

2.4. Organization and business processes

Since the last three years, the firm (report significant changes only):

- It has added new business processes/functions
- It has removed business processes/functions that are no longer needed
- It has introduced new technological skills (by hiring/training the employees)
- It has introduced new commercial skills (by hiring/training the employees)

- It has initiated training courses (within or outside the company) for the employees
- It has reorganized the business processes
- It has modified the hierarchy levels
- None of the previous answers

3.   BASIC DESCRIPTIVE STATISTICS

3.1   Changes in the Business Models

The information on business model changes collected through the survey provides some interesting descriptive evidence (Table A.2). First, we can see that firms mostly innovated their 'Products and production processes' area, as 32 per cent of the companies made at least one significant change in this area in the previous years. The second business model dimension that experienced relevant changes was 'Organization and business processes', with 29 per cent of companies adjusting this macro area. The 'Finance' function was less subject to BMI, as 23 per cent of the companies in the sample reconfigured their business model in this area. Finally, the 'Networks and relationships' category had the lowest percentage of companies making changes (19 per cent of companies in the sample); this can be attributable either to a stable network of partners, suppliers, or customers, suggesting that firms have already built strong relationships that require fewer adjustments, or to inherent difficulties in adapting existing networks to external contingencies.

Table A.2   Business model reconfiguration by area

Areas	%
Products and production processes	32%
Finance	23%
Networks and relationships	19%
Organization and business processes	29%

Source: Authors' elaboration of survey data.

Overall, the survey reveals that companies had a relatively stronger tendency to reconfigure the business model components related to 'Products and production processes' and 'Organization and business processes', while changes in the 'Finance' and 'Networks and relationships' domains were less frequent during the period under scrutiny.

Looking now at the business model components that were innovated in each of the four business model dimensions, we see that, in the 'Products and production processes' area, the most important changes made by the companies

mainly concern the introduction of new products or the addition of complementary services (48 per cent and 46 per cent of the companies, respectively).
Shortening time to market, on the other hand, seems to not be considered by
the companies as a decisive factor for a significant improvement of the adopted
business model. More detailed information on these business model changes
is shown in Table A.3.

Table A.3   *Products and production processes*

Areas	%
New products	48%
Introduction of accessory services	46%
Modification of the customer portfolio	36%
New production processes	35%
Product specialization	14%
Reduction of time to market	11%
No changes	16%

Source: Authors' elaboration of survey data.

In the Finance area (Table A.4), two clear trends emerge: on the one hand,
companies tended to focus on niche markets (37 per cent of companies) rather
than mass markets (4 per cent of companies). This shift can be attributed
to increased competition in mass markets, which makes it more difficult
for companies to differentiate themselves and maintain profitability. Niche
markets offer companies the opportunity to tailor their products or services to
meet specific customer needs, thus creating a unique position in the market.
On the other hand, companies preferred a dynamic pricing strategy (39 per
cent) over fixed pricing (15 per cent). Adopting dynamic pricing can be seen
as a response to ever-changing market conditions, fluctuations in demand, and
variable production costs. By making real-time price adjustments based on
factors such as supply and demand, competitor pricing and customer behaviour, companies can optimize their pricing strategies to maximize profits and
maintain competitiveness.

It is interesting to note that, while the sampled firms have made variations
to their pricing policies, the revenue model itself appears to have remained
unchanged. In addition, the introduction of complementary services has played
a crucial role in increasing company revenues, with 33 per cent of respondents
attributing their growth to this factor. Offering complementary services can
indeed increase customer value and diversify revenue streams. This strategic
move not only may attract new customers, but also foster loyalty among the
existing ones, leading to an increase in overall sales and revenues.

Table A.4   Finance

Areas	%
Dynamic price list	39%
Niche markets specialzation	37%
Higher revenue from new accessory services	33%
Changes in pricing policies	26%
Fixed price list	15%
Changes in revenue model	10%
Mass markets specialization	4%
No changes	17%

Source: Authors' elaboration of survey data.

Concerning 'Networks and relationships' (Table A.5), this business model dimension shows a clear prevalence of the introduction of new partnerships (reported by 41 per cent of the respondents). This highlights the growing importance of networks and strategic partnerships as a competitive element of business models. Looking at the data, Italian companies appear to rely primarily on direct channels (21 per cent of companies), which are preferred over indirect channels (14 per cent of companies). The integration of upstream or downstream production processes, on the other hand, seems to be marginal. Companies seem to prioritize their core activities and are more likely to seek 'servitization' or the introduction of new products related to their main product portfolio than to expand their upstream or downstream processes.

These findings underscore the preference of companies to build strong networks and form partnerships to improve their competitive position. The emphasis on direct sales channels reflects a deliberate choice to engage directly with customers, while 'servitization' and the expansion of the product portfolio indicate a focus on providing value-added services and core-related products to the market.

Table A.5   Networks and relationships

Areas	%
New partnerships	41%
Benefited from incentives for investments in innovation	26%
Introduced or modified direct sales channels	21%
Integration of accessory processes	15%
Process outsourcing	14%
Introduced or modified indirect sales channels	14%

Areas	%
Downstream process integration	11%
Upstream process integration	11%
No changes	25%

Source: Authors' elaboration of survey data.

Regarding the area 'Organization and business processes' (Table A.6), Italian companies have shown a preference for maintaining hierarchical levels (15 per cent of the sample) and for adding new business functions (34 per cent of companies). The skills of the new employees were technology-related, reflecting investment in digitization and Industry 4.0 initiatives. These advancements require technical rather than purely commercial skills, increasing the demand for tech-savvy professionals. In addition, 42 per cent of companies have implemented internal or external training courses, demonstrating their commitment to employee training. At the same time, 40 per cent of companies have significantly redesigned their internal processes to optimize them.

Table A.6   *Organization and business processes*

Areas	%
Implementation of training courses	42%
Process reconfiguration	40%
New technological skills	38%
New corporate functions	34%
New commercial skills	21%
Changes in hierarchical levels	15%
Elimination of corporate functions	14%
No changes	19%

Source: Authors' elaboration of survey data.

These trends highlight the efforts of Italian companies to strike a balance between continuity and adaptation of their organizational structures. By maintaining hierarchical levels and incorporating new functions, companies are attempting to maintain stability while responding to evolving market demands and technological advancements. The emphasis on technology-related skills is in line with the industry's shift toward digital transformation and leveraging the opportunities of Industry 4.0. In addition, the focus on training initiatives and process optimization underscores the companies' commitment to continuous improvement and adaptability. This strategic approach enables them to improve their overall capabilities and competitiveness in an increasingly dynamic business landscape.

All in all, the trends observed point to a proactive approach by Italian companies to remain resilient and flexible in a rapidly changing business environment. Their investment in capability development and process optimization reflects their commitment to sustainable growth and long-term success.

3.2   Adoption of Digital Technologies

The results of the survey suggest that Italian companies are still lagging behind in terms of adoption of new digital technologies. From Table A.7, for instance, we see that 62.16 per cent of the sampled companies had not introduced any digital technology yet at the time of the survey.

Table A.7   *Distribution of adopted technologies by firms (Italy)*

Technology adoption index	Number of firms	Percentage
0	2443	62.16
1	692	17.61
2	434	11.04
3	185	4.71
4	97	2.47
5	44	1.12
6	11	0.28
7	10	0.25
8	5	0.13
9	1	0.03
10	8	0.20
Total	3930	100.00

Source: Authors' elaboration of survey data.

More information is given in Figure A.3, which shows that the adoption rate of Industry 4.0 technologies ranges from 3 to 12 per cent, but it is steadily expanding. The focus of technology adoption lies primarily in areas such as Cloud Computing, Cybersecurity, and IoT, while the adoption rate for Cobots is comparatively lower. The market for these technologies seems undersized at present, but it shows potential for medium-term development (Figure A.4).

Figure A.5 analyses the relationship between the adoption rate and the planning rate for different technologies. Regarding Cobots, the planning rate exceeds the adoption rate, indicating a young and growing market segment. A similar situation can be observed for Augmented Reality, which is a devel-

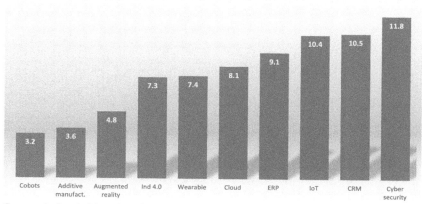

Source: Authors' elaboration of survey data.

Figure A.3   *Percentage of firms adopting Industry 4.0 technologies*

oping technology not yet widely adopted by Italian companies. On the other hand, Cybersecurity and Cloud Computing show a different pattern, with many Italian SMEs adopting these technologies. However, the data does not suggest market saturation, but rather a propensity for companies to invest in easily implementable technological fields.

Finally, Figure A.6 presents the ratio of the adoption rate to the expected demand expansion rate, calculated based on investment decisions declared by industry operators. The size of the circles represents the number of companies adopting the technology, with larger circles indicating a higher percentage of adoption. Technologies with a ratio lower than 1 (on the y-axis) exhibit higher planning rates than adoption rates, indicating potential developing markets in the medium term. IoT services, Cobots, and Augmented Reality are expected to benefit from a lively and growing market. The Cybersecurity and Cloud Computing markets appear to be more mature, but there is still significant demand potential in niche markets such as Data Breach analysis (Cybersecurity) and Blockchain (Cloud Computing), which have yet to be explored in the region.

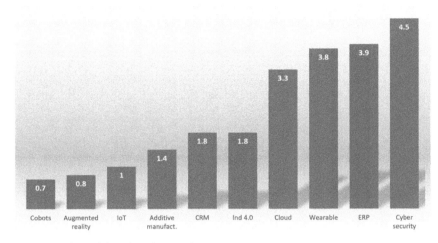

Source: Authors' elaboration of survey data.
Note: A ratio lower than one indicates a potential development of the technology.

Figure A.4   Technology adoption to planning ratio

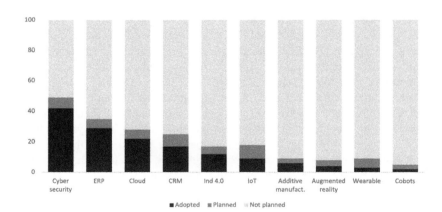

Source: Authors' elaboration of survey data.

Figure A.5   Industry 4.0 technology planning – adoption ratio (Italy)

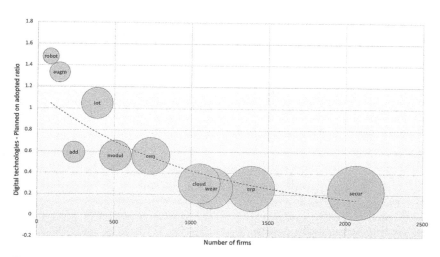

Source: Authors' elaboration of survey data.

Figure A.6   Adoption curve

Index